Using SPSS
for Social Statistics *and*
Research Methods

Using SPSS™
for Social Statistics *and*
Research Methods

William E. Wagner, III
California State University, Bakersfield

PINE FORGE PRESS
An Imprint of Sage Publications, Inc.
Thousand Oaks • London • New Delhi

For information:

Pine Forge Press
An imprint of SAGE Publications, Inc.
2455 Teller Road
Thousand Oaks, California 91320
E-mail: order@sagepub.com

SAGE Publications Ltd.
1 Oliver's Yard
55 City Road
London EC1Y 1SP
United Kingdom

SAGE Publications India Pvt. Ltd.
B-42, Panchsheel Enclave
Post Box 4109
New Delhi 110 017 India

Printed in the United States of America

Library of Congress Cataloging-in-Publication Data

Wagner, William E. (William Edward)
Using SPSS for social statistics and research methods / William E. Wagner, III.
    p. cm.
ISBN 1-4129-4077-X (pbk.)
    1. Social sciences—Statistical methods. 2. SPSS for Windows. I. Title.
HA32.W34 2007
300.285′555—dc22   2006007208

This book is printed on acid-free paper.

06   07   08   09   10   10   9   8   7   6   5   4   3   2   1

Acquiring Editor:	Jerry Westby
Editorial Assistant:	Kim Suarez
Production Editor:	Sanford Robinson
Copy Editor:	Cheryl Rivard
Typesetter:	C&M Digitals (P) Ltd.
Cover Designer:	Candice Harman

Contents

Preface

This book was written for anyone learning introductory statistics or with some basic statistics knowledge who wants to use SPSS software to manage data and/or carry out basic statistical analyses. It can also be a useful tool to gain an understanding of how SPSS works before going forward to more complicated statistical procedures. This volume is an ideal supplement for a statistics or research methods course. While it can be used with any research methods or statistics book or materials, it was tailored to complement *Investigating the Social World*, by Russell Schutt (Pine Forge Press), and *Social Statistics for a Diverse Society*, by Chava-Frankfort Nachmias and Anna Leon-Guerrero (Pine Forge Press). It can also be used as a guide for those working with basic statistics on their own. The book provides information for users about some of the important mechanics of SPSS operating procedures for simple data management along with accessible introductory statistical instructions.

Acknowledgments

Many thanks go to Jerry Westby at Pine Forge Press for his support and vision. Anna Leon-Guerrero and Russell Schutt were particularly helpful, providing insightful reviews and productive suggestions. Gratitude also goes to Curt Raney, PhD, at St. Mary's College of Maryland. I first learned about and used SPSS in his Data Analysis class.

For my sister, Becky, & my brother, Ben . . .

1

Overview

This book will serve as a guide for those interested in using SPSS software to aid in statistical data analysis, whether as a companion to a statistics or research methods course or as a stand-alone guide. The images and directions used in this book come from SPSS version 14.0, released in the fall of 2005. This manual can be used to supplement a statistics or research methods class and/or textbook, or it can be used as a stand-alone guide to aid in the process of data analysis.

The SPSS software works with several kinds of computer files: data files, output files, and syntax files. Data files are those computer files that contain the information that the user wants to statistically analyze. Output files contain the statistical analysis and often tables, graphs, and/or charts. Syntax files are computer instructions that tell the SPSS software what to do. Syntax files are not used in the student version of the SPSS software and are dealt with as an advanced application in Chapter 9 of this book.

The General Social Survey (GSS) will be the secondary data set used as an example to demonstrate typical functions of the program. While SPSS is the software program, produced by SPSS Inc., of Chicago, Illinois, the General Social Survey (GSS) is a data set that is read and analyzed by the SPSS software; it is a data file containing the information to be analyzed. The two things are distinct and can be used in separate contexts without the other.

SPSS uses different file extensions, or *endings,* and associated icons to signify types of files. For instance, a file named "file.sav" is a data file called "file." The ".sav" is used to signify that this is a data file. Again, data files contain the information that SPSS is used to analyze. A file with the extension ".sps" is an SPSS syntax file, while a file with the extension ".spo" is an SPSS output file. Output files contain SPSS analysis and such things as charts, tables, and other information. Syntax files contain coded instructions for SPSS to perform operations on data and to produce output. It is not necessary to create, save, or even deal with syntax files for most basic SPSS functions; therefore, syntax files will be covered only to the level of description in Chapter 9.

Opening Existing Data Files

In order to open an SPSS data file that you already have or have obtained, select the "File" menu, then choose "Open" and select "Data." (For other file types, see the section on importing data from non-SPSS file formats.) At this point, you will need to navigate the disk drives (or network drives or other sorts of storage devices) to locate the data file that you wish to open. Once you locate the file, either double-click it, or click it once and click the "Open" key toward the bottom right side of the "Open File" dialog box.

SPSS will then open the data file and you will be presented with the information in a grid format. You have choices both about the way the information is presented and about the information that you see. For example, you can choose the "Data View," presented in the following image. Note that the variables are listed in columns with each case recorded as a row. The variable "age" has been selected as a reference point. The data in that column tell the ages of each of the respondents.

Now click on the "Variable View" tab, which is located toward the bottom left of the screen. While the information looks somewhat different, you are still looking at the same data file. See the following image.

Again, the "age" variable has been selected for reference. In this view, variables are depicted in rows, and information about the variables is included,

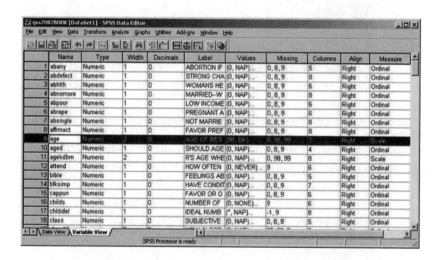

such as variable label, category labels, type, level of measurement, and so on. You can add to, edit, or delete any of the variable information contained in this view by directly typing into the cells. This view does not show the actual response data, as is shown in the "Data View" option.

Importing Data From Non-SPSS File Formats

There is often a need to analyze existing data files that were not created or formatted by SPSS software. These files might be created by other statistical software packages (e.g., SAS) or by other types of numeric programs (e.g., Microsoft Excel). To open these files, first select the same menu options you would as if you were opening an SPSS data file:

FILE → OPEN → DATA

Now, at the "Files of type" prompt at the bottom of the dialog box, click the arrow at the right to expand the choices. Next, select "Excel (*.xls)." You will need to navigate your hard drive, other drives, or locations to find your file. Once you do, select and open it. At this point, you will be presented with a new dialog box.

If the column headings in the Microsoft Excel file contain the variable names, then make sure the box asking to "Read variable names from the first row of data" is selected. If the column headings are not formatted in a way that conforms to the SPSS variable-naming conventions, then they will be transformed into permitted variable names and the original names will be recorded as variable labels.

To import only a portion of the Excel file, then enter the range of cells from which you would like to import data.

It is also possible to import files from databases, text files, and other sources. Follow the same instructions as with Excel files, except for the file type you select. Depending on the file type you choose, you will be presented with different dialog boxes or wizards to import the data.

In some cases, you may simply have unlabeled data in a particular file, or the variable names or other information may be of little or no use to you. In that case, depending on the size of the file, you could copy the data from the original numeric program (e.g., Microsoft Excel) and then paste it directly into the SPSS "Data View" window. This is particularly useful if you just want to add numeric values from another source and enter or program the other information using SPSS.

Opening Previously Created Output Files

In order to open a previously created output file, select from the "File" menu as follows.

FILE → OPEN → OUTPUT

You will be presented with the following dialog box:

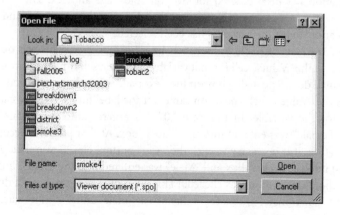

Here, just navigate to find your file, as you would any other type of file. Once you locate it, select and open the file. SPSS will open the file into an "Output Viewer" window. There, you can view and edit it.

Saving Files

Saving any type of SPSS file is performed in virtually the same way as with any modern computer program. Select either:

FILE → SAVE   To save the file as the currently assigned name

or

FILE → SAVE AS   To save the file in a different file, under a new name

The first option above will automatically save the file without prompting you for a dialog box, unless you are working with a new, yet unnamed file. In that case, you will get the same type of dialog box as if you had selected the "Save As" option. If you do choose the second option, you will be given a dialog box prompting you to name the file and to select the location on your computer or network where the file is to be placed.

Creating New SPSS Data Files

To create a new SPSS data file, select the "File" menu, then choose "New" and select "Data."

FILE → NEW → DATA

You will be given a blank "Data Editor" window. One can immediately start entering information about the variables you wish to create and/or the actual data codes that you may have. In the "Data Editor" window that follows, information has been entered for two variables: age and sex. The "Variable View" tab has been selected. Notice that the labels have been entered, and other information about the variables has been selected.

For the "sex" variable, value labels have been entered. This was done by clicking on the "Values" cell for that variable and then selecting the button with three small dots. The dialog box on the next page would have appeared.

In the "Value Labels" box, you can enter the label for each of the category codes for the variable. In this case, "0" was entered into the "Value" box, while "Female" was entered into the "Label" box. At that point, to record the information, it is necessary to click the "Add" button. Notice also that "1" was entered into the "Value" box and "Male" was entered into the "Label" box, and again, the "Add" button was clicked. (This procedure also produces a dummy variable called "male," where the value of 1 is "male" and 0 is "not male.")

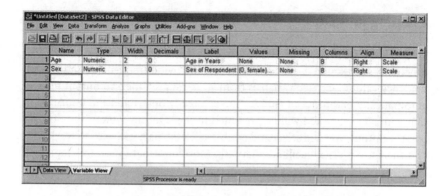

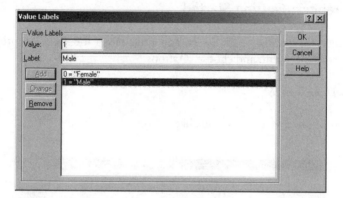

It is also possible to enter the data directly into the Data Editor. To do this, click the "Data View" tab at the lower left of the "Data Editor" window. The columns now represent the newly created variables: age and sex.

Creating and Editing SPSS Output Files

Output files are created by SPSS when you instruct the software to perform functions. For example, if you ask SPSS to provide frequencies and central tendency values for three variables from your data set, then an output file will automatically be produced (unless one is already open) and the information that you have requested will be presented in the "Output Viewer" window. To edit the output, you will select and double-click the part you wish to work with and there are tools to facilitate that task. More information on this topic will be provided in Chapter 2: "Organization and Presentation of Information."

Preferences: Getting Started

To change the settings, parameters, and preferences for the SPSS program, select the "Edit" menu and choose "Options."

EDIT→ OPTIONS

You will be given a dialog box like the one shown here:

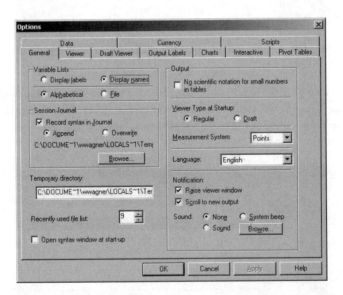

There are numerous features that can be controlled using this dialog box, and most are intuitive in their operation. As a user becomes more experienced, she or he often uses more of these features. From the start, however, most SPSS users will want to make sure that variables will be displayed throughout the program in alphabetical order and by name. This can be done by selecting the "General" tab and clicking the radio buttons for "Display names" and "Alphabetical."

This is particularly important if you are using or creating a data set that contains a large number of variables, such as the General Social Survey. While it is clear that alphabetizing the list will facilitate easier access to variables, listing by name is also crucial since variable labels are more detailed and may not necessarily begin with or even use the same letters as the variable name. Changing or verifying these settings up front can save a good deal of time and frustration. If a data set is opened and the preferences have not been set to the desired parameters, the user can still go to the dialog box and make the change while the data set is open. (In some older versions of SPSS, it was necessary to close the data set, make the change, and reopen the data set.)

To get a quick overview of the variables in a given data set, SPSS has a variable utility window to provide useful information about each of the variables in a way that can be easily navigated (and so that the information can be easily pasted to output if desired). By opening this window, the importance of organized naming and ordering of variables in a large data file can be exemplified. Choose the "Utilities" menu, then select "Variables."

UTILITIES → VARIABLES

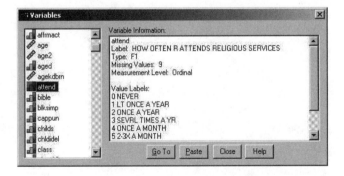

When selecting a variable from the alphabetized list of variable names on the left, information about that particular variable will appear on the right side of the box, including the label, level of measurement, and value labels. This is a fast way to determine what kind of variables are available in your data set that are suited to different statistical methods of analysis.

Measurement of Variables Using SPSS

Whether creating a new data file with SPSS or using an existing data file, it is important to understand how variables have been measured, or "treated," by the creator of the data file. This "treatment" is a factor of how the data were collected—how much information is contained within the data set about a variable.

First, it is important to be aware that SPSS can record variables as either *string* variables or *numeric* variables. String variables can consist of letters and/or numbers and cannot be treated numerically; therefore, string variables must be treated at the nominal level of measurement. Numeric variables use numbers to represent response values. These numbers may represent actual numbers, ranked categories, or unranked categories. In other words, numeric variables may be nominal, ordinal, interval, or ratio.

In social science statistics and research methods courses, variables are typically described as nominal, ordinal, interval, or ratio. Many textbooks, such as *Investigating the Social World* (2004, 4th ed.), by Russell Schutt, elaborate all four of these categories. In some texts, interval and ratio measures are combined, as is the case in *Social Statistics for a Diverse Society* (2006, 4th ed.), by Chava Frankfort-Nachmias and Anna Leon-Guerrero.

SPSS uses three codes for levels of measurement: nominal, ordinal, and scale. Nominal and ordinal both correspond to the concepts with the same names. Scale corresponds with interval-ratio, interval, and ratio.

2

Transforming Variables

I n this chapter, tools for restructuring variables will be introduced. SPSS allows for numerous ways to reconfigure, combine, and compute variable data.

Recoding and Computing Variables

Often, one must reorganize the way data are recorded before performing statistical analyses. This might be due to the level of measurement of a particular variable that a researcher wishes to change, or it may be related to the researcher's intended use of a variable. "Recoding" is the SPSS function that allows the researcher to recategorize the variable to suit the needs of the analysis.

There are many times when a researcher needs to produce a new variable from existing information in a data set, but that information is not entirely contained within one variable. SPSS has a "Compute" function that allows a user to both perform mathematical operations on variable data and combine data from multiple variable sources.

RECODING VARIABLES

For our recoding example, we will use the General Social Survey (GSS), 2002, data set. We will take a straightforward case of dichotomizing age from a ratio variable presenting the respondent's actual age at the time of interview into just two categories with a cut point of 50 years of age. In order to recode, or change the categories of, a variable, select the "Transform" menu, then choose the "Recode" option, and then select "Into Different Variables."

TRANSFORM → RECODE → INTO DIFFERENT VARIABLES

You will then be given a dialog box like the one displayed here:

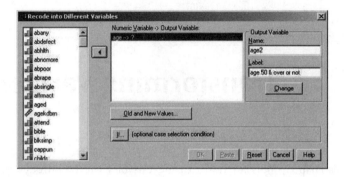

It is a good idea to code into "different variables" rather than same variables if you are reducing information contained within the data. For instance, if you are recoding a ratio-level variable into an ordinal or a dichotomous variable, then you would want to create a different variable. The reason for this is that the lost information resulting from the recode would still be retained in the original variable should you want to change the way in which you recode the variable later, or should you need the more detailed ratio information.

In this example, we recode age into a dichotomy. Select "age" from the list of variables in the data set on the left, then click the arrow to move it to the "Numeric Variable" slot. Now, create a new name for the variable; in this example, the mundane "age2" has been used. You may also select a label at this time, or you can attend to that at a later time through the variable view screen. In this instance, the label "age 50 & over or not" was chosen. While it hasn't been done yet in the screen image, the next step is to click the "Change" key. This will enter the name "age2" into the "Output Variable" slot.

Now it is necessary to give SPSS the instructions for *how* to recode the variable. In this example, we want to change all ages up to and including 49 into a category, call it "0," and all ages 50 and greater into another category, call it "1." Click on the "Old and New Values" key in the dialog box and another dialog box will appear on top, like the one on the next page.

To implement the changes, first, under "Old Value," select the radio button that reads "Range, LOWEST through value." Enter "49" here. Then under "New Value," select "Value" and enter "0." Now click the "Add" key. This instructs SPSS to transform all ages up to and including 49 into category 0.

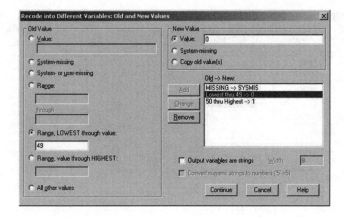

Next, under "Old Value," select the radio button associated with "Range, value through Highest." Enter 50 in the box beneath that heading. Then under "New Value," select "Value" and enter "1." Again, click the "Add" key. This now instructs SPSS to transform all ages 50 and above into category 1.

Next, under "Old Value," select "System- or user-missing." Under "New Value," select "System-missing." This will ensure that missing values continue to be treated as such, even if they had been recorded as numeric values. Click the "Add" key once again.

Now the instructions have been entered and you can click the "Continue" key that will close this box and return you to the original "Recode into Different Variables" dialog box. Once there, you must click the "OK" key for SPSS to process your request to recode and then create the new variable.

If the "OK" is dimmed and SPSS will not allow you to click it, then one of the above steps must not have been completed. The one most often overlooked is clicking on the "Change" key.

Notice that the new variable is appended to the bottom of the variable list in the "Variable View" of the "Data Editor" window. You can move that variable to another place in the list if you wish by selecting it, then dragging it between two of the other variables.

Since this is a newly created variable, it is very important to insert value labels. If the variable label is not clear, then it can be easy to forget what the values are or in which direction the variable was coded.

As before with value labels, enter both the value and the label. Then click "Add" after each pair of typed information. Then click "OK." The value labels will then be updated.

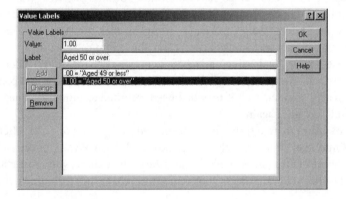

COMPUTING VARIABLES

There are many reasons why a user of SPSS would be interested in computing a new variable. For example, one may want to construct an index from individual questions, or one may wish to compute the log function of a particular variable. In this example, we want to compute the average education level of the respondent's parents. So we will add the mother's education level to the father's education level and then divide by two. (In more sophisticated situations, we might divide by the number of parental responses.)

To perform the computation, select these menus:

FILE → TRANSFORM → COMPUTE

The "Compute Variable" dialog box will be presented.

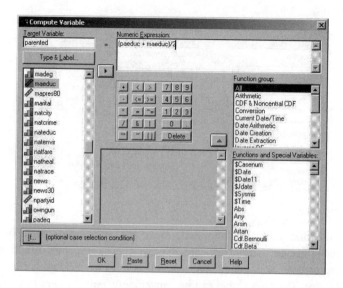

Type the name you wish to assign to the new variable in the "Target Variable" box. Next, prepare the computation equation in the "Numeric Expression" box. In this case, it's necessary to select the parentheses, ( ), first. Then insert the "maeduc" and an addition sign, followed by the "paeduc" variable, into the parentheses. Now put a divisor bar and click the number "2." This has the effect of adding together the total years of education of both parents and dividing by two, leaving the average.

Note the functions that are available to use. There are statistical, trigonometric, date, time, string, and so on functions that can be used to compute just about anything. Also, if you want to set up a conditional computation—such that a computation is only made in one case, or there are to be different computations for different cases, based on some predetermined condition, then select the "If" button, and enter the condition(s). The same functions and keypads are provided to instruct SPSS how to determine the criteria for the conditional computation.

USING THE COUNT FUNCTION

SPSS allows users the option to add up particular values across variables. Suppose a researcher wanted to count up the number of instances where a respondent gave a "yes" answer to particular questions. For this example, consider the GSS series of questions on opinions relating to abortion. Use the menus below to carry out this example:

TRANSFORM → COUNT . . .

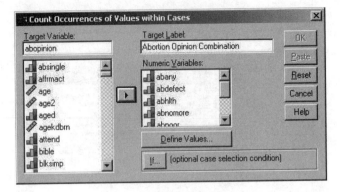

In the dialog box that appears, move the appropriate variables from the variable list on the left into the "Numeric Variables" box. It will also be necessary to enter a name for the new variable to be created in the "Target Variable" slot. The target label can be conveniently entered here as well. Next, click the "Define Values" button. The following dialog box will be provided:

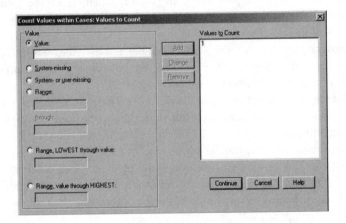

Here, you will want to select the values to be counted. For the opinion questions that have been selected in this example, a code of 1 indicates an affirmative response (while a 2 indicates a negative response). Therefore, we want to count the number of questions with a 1. Click the radio button next to "Value" at the upper left of the dialog box, then enter a "1" into the associated slot. Now click the "Add" key on the right side of the dialog box. The "1" should appear in the "Values to Count" area. Now click the "Continue" key in this box, and then the "OK" key in the prior dialog box. While output will not be generated, a new variable will be created. See the following screen image for the data contained within the new variable that has been created.

	npartyid	inccod98	age2	rrace	male	abopinion	var	var
1	3	82500	.00	1.00	1.00	6.00		
2	2	45000	.00	1.00	1.00	.00		
3	3	67500	.00	1.00	1.00	2.00		
4	3	55000	1.00	1.00	1.00	.00		
5	3	110000	.00	1.00	1.00	.00		
6	3	45000	.00	1.00	1.00	.00		
7	4	27500	.00	1.00	1.00	.00		
8	1	55000	.00	.00	1.00	.00		
9	1	32500	1.00	1.00	1.00	3.00		
10	1	82500	1.00	1.00	1.00	3.00		
11	4	97	.00	1.00	1.00	.00		
12	1	500	.00	1.00	1.00	.00		
13	3	0	1.00	1.00	1.00	6.00		
14	3	18750	1.00	1.00	1.00	6.00		
15	2	27500	.00	1.00	1.00	.00		
16	3	37500	.00	1.00	1.00	1.00		
17	3	67500	.00	1.00	1.00	.00		
18	3	13750	1.00	1.00	1.00	3.00		
19	3	0	1.00	1.00	1.00	.00		
20	1	0	1.00	2.00	1.00	.00		
21	1	18750	.00	2.00	1.00	.00		
22	2	55000	.00	1.00	1.00	.00		
23	2	45000	.00	1.00	1.00	.00		
24	2	32500	.00	1.00	1.00	.00		
25	1	0	1.00	1.00	1.00	.00		
26	1	110000	1.00	1.00	1.00	.00		
27	1	0	.00	.00	1.00	.00		
28	4	45000	1.00	1.00	1.00	.00		
29	3	11750	.00	1.00	1.00	1.00		

COMPUTING AN INDEX USING MEAN

It is possible to construct an index using the "Compute" command in SPSS. The most direct way of doing this is to use the "Mean" function. To use this method, click these menus:

TRANSFORM → COMPUTE . . .

When presented with the "Compute Variable" dialog box, select "Mean" from the "Functions and Special Variables" box in the lower right corner. Make sure "Function group" is set to "All." After you select "Mean," click the up-arrow

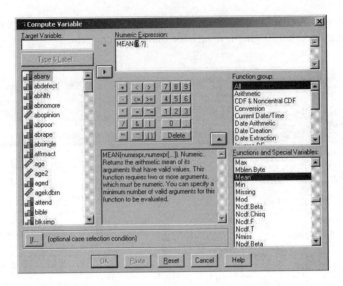

sending "Mean" to the "Numeric Expression" area. It will appear as it does in the image above. You must insert all of the variables of interest within the parentheses, each separated by a comma. See the following dialog box for how this is done in the current example.

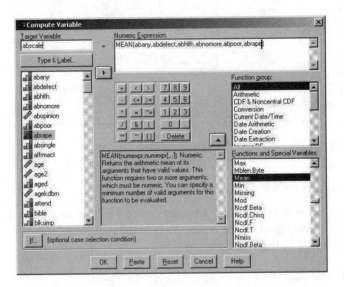

After selecting the variables from the bank on the left, enter the target variable (new variable to be created) name. Then click the "Type & Label" button. The following short dialog box will be provided:

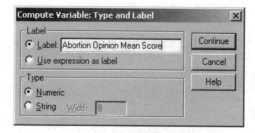

Click the radio button next to "Label" and enter the appropriate variable label in the adjacent slot. Now click "Continue," then "OK." A new variable, "abscale," will be created and appear in the SPSS "Data Editor" window as shown below.

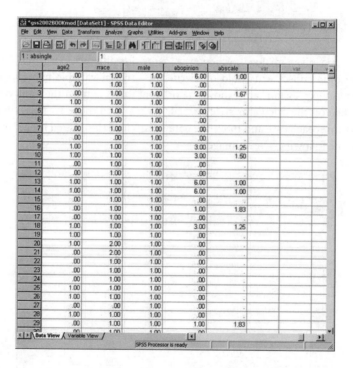

In this case, for nonmissing data, notice that the value computed for the mean falls between (and including) 1 and 2. This is because 1 represents "yes" and 2 represents "no." For statistical purposes, it is sometimes beneficial to have a result between 0 and 1 instead. To arrange for this, you could also subtract the number 1 from the completed mean function in the original compute box, or you can go back now and make the change exhibited as follows. Again click these menus:

TRANSFORM → COMPUTE . . .

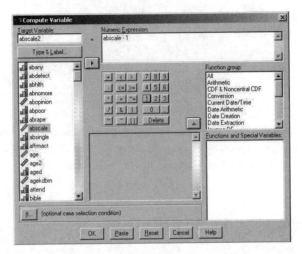

In the given dialog box, enter a name for the new variable. (While not recommended, you could overwrite the original variable name.) In the "Numeric Expression" area, move the original variable from the bank on the left. Then on the calculator-style keypad, click "-" and then "1." This will subtract 1 from each case and move the data means into the desired range, as they are in the following screen image.

	age2	rrace	male	abopinion	abscale	abscale2	var
1	.00	1.00	1.00	6.00	1.00	.00	
2	.00	1.00	1.00	.00			
3	.00	1.00	1.00	2.00	1.67	.67	
4	1.00	1.00	1.00	.00			
5	.00	1.00	1.00	.00			
6	.00	1.00	1.00	.00			
7	.00	1.00	1.00	.00			
8	.00	.00	1.00	.00			
9	1.00	1.00	1.00	3.00	1.25	.25	
10	1.00	1.00	1.00	3.00	1.50	.50	
11	.00	1.00	1.00	.00			
12	.00	1.00	1.00	.00			
13	1.00	1.00	1.00	6.00	1.00	.00	
14	1.00	1.00	1.00	6.00	1.00	.00	
15	.00	1.00	1.00	.00			
16	.00	1.00	1.00	1.00	1.83	.83	
17	.00	1.00	1.00	.00			
18	1.00	1.00	1.00	3.00	1.25	.25	
19	1.00	1.00	1.00	.00			
20	1.00	2.00	1.00	.00			
21	.00	2.00	1.00	.00			
22	.00	1.00	1.00	.00			
23	.00	1.00	1.00	.00			
24	.00	1.00	1.00	.00			
25	1.00	1.00	1.00	.00			
26	1.00	1.00	1.00	.00			
27	.00	.00	1.00	.00			
28	1.00	1.00	1.00	.00			
29	.00	1.00	1.00	1.00	1.83	.83	

MULTIPLE RESPONSE

To produce multiple response values (e.g., frequency values combined across multiple variables), choose the following menus:

ANALYZE → MULTIPLE RESPONSE → DEFINE SETS . . .

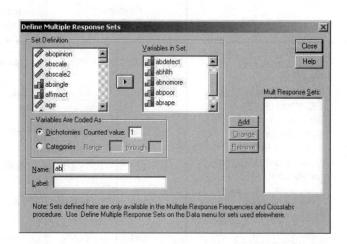

From the variable bank on the left, move all of the desired variables into the "Variables in Set" box. In this example, the variables chosen are dichotomies and we are counting the "yes" value, 1. It is also possible to select a category and range. Now name the set and type the name in the "Name" slot. You also have the opportunity to place a label at this time as well. Finally, click the "Add" key on the right side of the dialog box. You can now click "Close."

In order to produce a frequency table for the response set that has just been identified, click the following menus:

ANALYZE → MULTIPLE RESPONSE → FREQUENCIES . . .

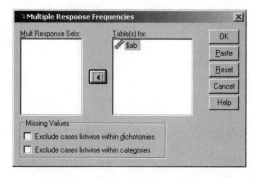

Select the response set from the list on the left (in this case, it was the only item in the list). Move the set to the "Tables for" box. Then click "OK." SPSS will produce output like the following:

$ab Frequencies

		Responses		Percent of Cases
		N	Percent	
$ab [a]	ABORTION IF WOMAN WANTS FOR ANY REASON	208	11.2%	45.4%
	STRONG CHANCE OF SERIOUS DEFECT	383	20.6%	83.6%
	WOMANS HEALTH SERIOUSLY ENDANGERED	446	24.0%	97.4%
	MARRIED–WANTS NO MORE CHILDREN	213	11.4%	46.5%
	LOW INCOME–CANT AFFORD MORE CHILDREN	221	11.9%	48.3%
	PREGNANT AS RESULT OF RAPE	391	21.0%	85.4%
Total		1862	100.0%	406.6%

[a.] Dichotomy group tabulated at value1.

Note that the multiple response command allows easy production of a table combining similar-style variables counting a particular category or range. In the screen image above, it is easy to see the similarities and differences in percentages of those who support abortion in the listed circumstances.

3

Organization and Presentation of Information

In this chapter, basic methods of data description will be exhibited. This information will include frequency distributions, measures of central tendency, and measures of variability. Presentation can be made in table, chart, or graph form.

Measures of Central Tendency and Variability

In order to quickly produce a table with basic descriptive statistics about a variable or variables, select the following menus:

ANALYZE → DESCRIPTIVES → DESCRIPTIVES

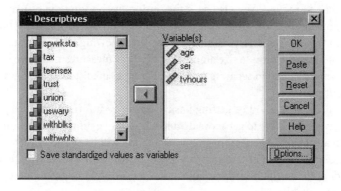

By clicking on the "Options" button at the lower right-hand corner of the "Descriptives" dialog box, you will be given another dialog box that will allow you to choose which basic descriptive information will be produced by SPSS.

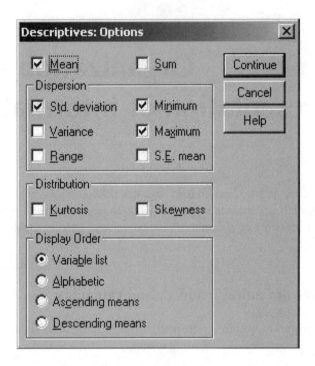

Select the boxes, leaving a check mark next to those statistics that you would like to request. You also have the option of choosing the display order; choose one of the four options. After clicking "Continue" in this dialog box and "OK" in the original one, you will be given the following SPSS output.

Note that the sample size along with the four measures that were selected have been presented in separate columns. Variables are listed in the rows of the table output.

While that method of getting basic descriptive information is very quick and easy, it is possible to get more detailed descriptive information about variables in a data set. Note that the previous method will NOT allow you to obtain the median. One can obtain information about measures of central tendency (*including the median*) and variability, as well as obtaining actual frequency distribution tables.

Descriptive Statistics

	N	Minimum	Maximum	Mean	Std. Deviation
AGE OF RESPONDENT	1	1	8	4	17.45
	496	8	9	6.21	4
RESPONDENT	1	1	9	4	19.18
SOCIOECONOMIC INDEX	426	7.1	7.2	8.974	13
HOURS PER DAY	5		2	3.	2.385
WATCHING TV	01	0	2	06	
Valid N (listwise)	4				
	75				

FREQUENCY DISTRIBUTIONS

Using the same variables as in the previous example, select the following menus:

ANALYZE → DESCRIPTIVES → FREQUENCIES . . .

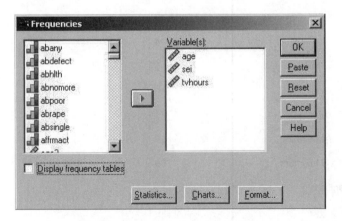

For now, make sure that the "Display frequency tables" box is *unchecked*. The three selected variables, "age," "sei," and "tvhours," are all scale variables. Therefore, the frequency distribution tables would have too many categories and be too long to be of any real use. One must be cognizant of the level of measurement and categorization of variables before selecting tables.

To choose which statistical information to request, click the "Statistics" button and you will be presented with the preceding dialog box.

Here, you can choose measures of central tendency (mean, median, and/or mode) and measures of variability. Quartiles are useful for computing the IQR (interquartile range). You can also select any percentile for computation, as well, depending on your specific needs. Based on the above dialog boxes, the following output will be provided once you click "Continue," then "OK" in the original dialog box.

Statistics

		AGE OF RESPONDENT	RESPONDENT SOCIOECONOMIC INDEX	HOURS PER DAY WATCHING TV
N	Valid	140	1426	501
	Missing	4	74	999
Mean		46.21	48.974	3.06
Median		44.00	41.600	2.00
Mode		34	63.5	2
Std. Deviation		17.454	19.1813	2.385
Variance		304.640	367.924	5.688
Range		71	80.1	22
Minimum		18	17.1	0
Maximum		89	97.2	22
Percentiles	25	32.00	33.100	2.00
	50	44.00	41.600	2.00
	75	58.75	63.500	4.00

Now perform the same menu function with a different variable.

ANALYZE → DESCRIPTIVES → FREQUENCIES . . .

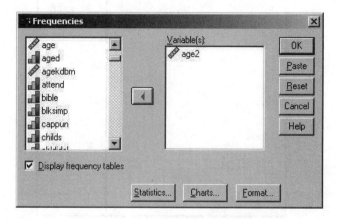

First, remove the variables that were there by clicking the "Reset" button. Now select "age2," the recoded age dichotomy variable, and move it into the "Variable(s)" box. Click the "Charts" button. You will be given a subdialog box as follows:

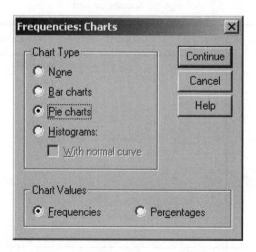

Choose the "Pie charts" radio button and "Frequencies." (Of course, depending on your needs, and the level of measurement of your variable(s), you could select any of these types of charts.) Then click "Continue," then "OK" in the original dialog box. The following information represents the output that SPSS will provide.

Statistics

age 50 & over or not

N	Valid	1496
	Missing	4
Mean		.3951
Median		.0000
Mode		.00
Std. Deviation		.48903
Variance		.239

age 50 & over or not

		Frequency	Percent	Valid Percent	Cumulative Percent
Valid	.00	905	60.3	60.5	60.5
	1.00	591	39.4	39.5	100.0
	Total	1496	99.7	100.0	
Missing	System	4	.3		
Total		1500	100.0		

age 50 & over or not

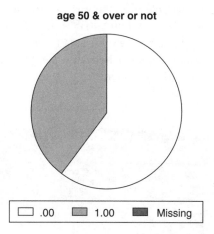

    .00   1.00   Missing

While this is one way to obtain some of the chart and graph options, there are more detailed options and optimized interfaces for producing charts and graphs, which are explained in Chapter 4, "Charts and Graphs."

Suppose that you want to produce a frequency distribution for age beyond just the dichotomy that was demonstrated in the previous example. It is not feasible to run the frequency command/menus using age, since a virtually useless table listing all ages in the data file will be generated.

In order to present a useful frequency distribution, it makes sense to divide the interval-ratio variable, age, into meaningful or otherwise appropriate categories. Take, for instance, the following example where age is divided into ranges according to decade. Bear in mind that the GSS (General Social Survey) contains responses only from those 18 years of age and above. First, use the following menus to recode age into "agegroup" (see Chapter 2 for more detail on recoding):

TRANSFORM → RECODE → INTO DIFFERENT VARIABLES . . .

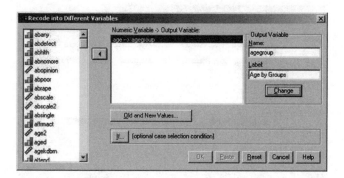

Select the original variable from the variable list on the left and move it into the "Numeric Variable -> Output Variable" area. On the right side of the dialog box, be sure to name the new variable (here, the new name is "agegroup") and provide a label if desired. Now click the "Old and New Values" key. The following dialog box will be presented:

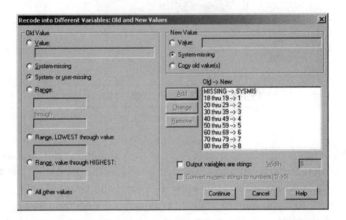

Here, enter the old values and ranges on the left in conjunction with the new value on the right, clicking "Add" after each entry. For more details, review the recoding section of Chapter 2. After all of the old and new values have been keyed in, click "Continue" here, then "OK" in the previous dialog box. The new variable will be displayed in the SPSS "Data Editor" window.

Click the "Variable View" tab and find the newly created variable. In the "Values" cell, click the button with three dots. You will be given the following dialog box:

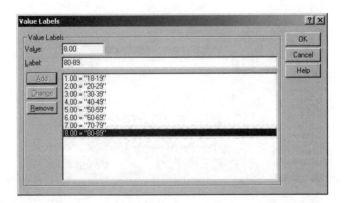

Enter the appropriate labels, as done in the example above. Then click "OK." This will record the labels onto the variable.

Next, request a frequency distribution for the newly structured variable. To do so, click the following menus:

ANALYZE → DESCRIPTIVE STATISTICS → FREQUENCIES . . .

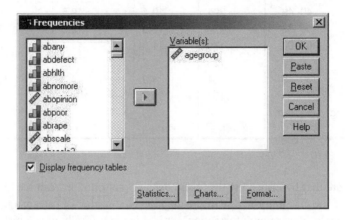

When given the above dialog box, move the variable of interest from the list on the left into the "Variable(s)" box. (For a visual representation of the distribution, select the "Charts . . ." button and see the dialog box that follows.)

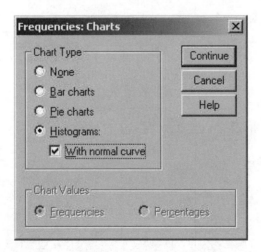

Click the radio button next to "Histograms" and check the box for "With normal curve." This will produce a histogram with an overlay of a normal curve for reference. Click "Continue" here, then click "OK" in the prior dialog box. SPSS will generate the following output consisting of an easy-to-understand frequency table and a histogram.

Age by Groups

		Frequency	Percent	Valid Percent	Cumulative Percent
Valid	18–19	16	1.1	1.1	1.1
	20–29	275	18.3	18.4	19.5
	30–39	323	21.5	21.6	41.0
	40–49	291	19.4	19.5	60.5
	50–59	234	15.6	15.6	76.1
	60–69	170	11.3	11.4	87.5
	70–79	123	8.2	8.2	95.7
	80–89	64	4.3	4.3	100.0
	Total	1496	99.7	100.0	
Missing	System	4	.3		
Total		1500	100.0		

Note that by inspecting the "Valid Percent" column, one can readily get a sense of the distribution, due to the manageable number of categories (rows) in the table. This same information is provided graphically in the histogram that follows.

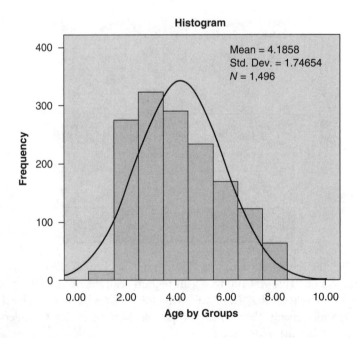

Histogram

Mean = 4.1858
Std. Dev. = 1.74654
N = 1,496

4

Charts and Graphs

I n this chapter, the techniques for producing a number of useful graphics will be explained. There are a number of other chart and graph options that are not explained in this section, although they are contained within the "Graph" menu and can be explored with knowledge of how to use the other SPSS graph functions along with statistical and research methods background.

Most of the charts and graphs discussed in this section, as well as those not covered in this book, can be "double-clicked" in the Output Editor. After double-clicking, the object opens in a new window that allows editing of text, colors, graphics, additions of other features, and even other variables.

From the SPSS Editor window, the graphs, charts, and tables that are produced can be selected and copied (Control + C or Apple + C) then pasted (Control + V or Apple + V) into a word-processing program like Microsoft Word.

Boxplot

A boxplot is a visual representation of the frequency distribution of a variable showing shape, central tendency, and variability of a distribution. It can also be called a box-and-whiskers diagram. To produce a boxplot:

GRAPHS → BOXPLOT . . .

In this example, we will draw a simple boxplot for one variable, age. Click "Simple" and select the button for "Summaries of separate variables." Then click the "Define" button. You will be given another dialog box.

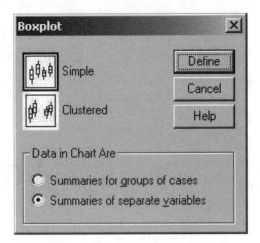

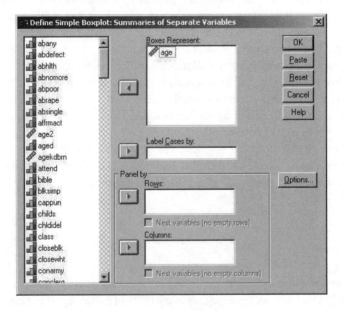

In this dialog box, move the variable(s) of interest into the "Boxes Represent" location. Click "OK" and SPSS will provide the boxplot(s) that you have requested as shown in the following image. Information about the distribution is contained in the boxplot.

The upper and lower boundaries of the box represent Q3 (75th percentile) and Q1 (25th percentile), respectively. Values correspond to the scale on the left axis of the figure. Therefore, the box itself shows the IQR (interquartile range). The line inside the box is drawn at the 50th percentile. The lines extending above and below the box are referred to as whiskers. At the end of the top whisker, the maximum score is marked. The minimum value can be found at the end of the lower whisker.

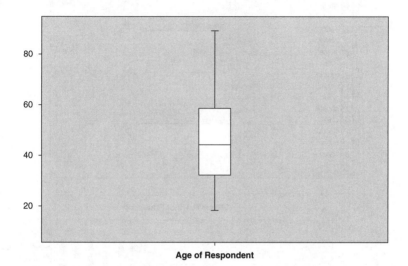

Age of Respondent

SOURCE: General Social Survey, 2002.[1]

Scatterplot

A scatterplot is a useful graph to display the relationship between two scale, or interval-ratio, variables. To create a scatterplot, use these menu directions:

GRAPHS → SCATTERPLOT . . .

Select variables for the X- and Y-axes. In this example, "SEI" (socioeconomic status) has been selected for the Y-axis (dependent variable), and "Years of Education" has been chosen for the X-axis (independent variable).

In the graph for "SEI by Years of Education," there does appear to be an upward trend. Note also that the data points all fall along vertical lines due to the nature of the variable education, which has been categorized into discrete number of years (not allowing for 13.5 years, for instance). In the case of a true continuously measured variable, those distinct vertical lines would not show up in the scatterplot.

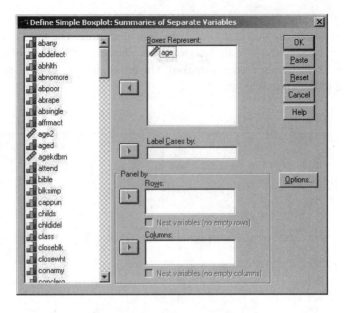

SEI by Years of Education

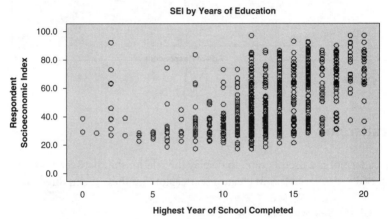

SOURCE: General Social Survey, 2002.[1]

Histogram

In order to display a graphic representation of the distribution of a single scale variable, the histogram serves well. This is a bar graph that can be used with variables at the interval and ratio levels. The bars touch. The width of the bars represents the width of the intervals, and the height of the bars represents the frequency of each interval. To create a histogram, follow the menus:

GRAPHS → HISTOGRAM . . .

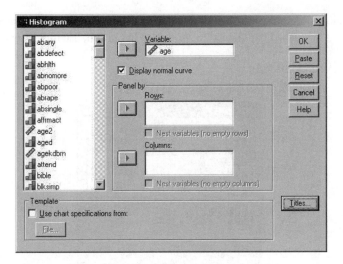

In the "Histogram" dialog box, select the variable of interest. In this case, age was chosen. The SPSS output is shown as follows:

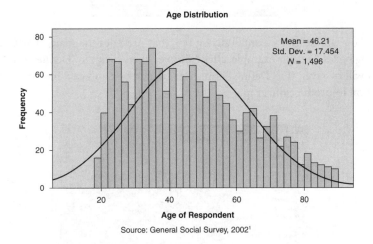

The histogram is displayed with an overlay of a normal curve.

Bar Graph

Usage of bar graphs is common and varied. SPSS provides many ways of using bar graphs to illustrate information. Much like in Microsoft Excel, or other spreadsheet and data graphics programs, SPSS produces bar charts in a number of different ways. It is possible to create standard bar charts, as well as clustered or stacked bar charts. To produce a bar graph, use these menus:

GRAPHS → BAR

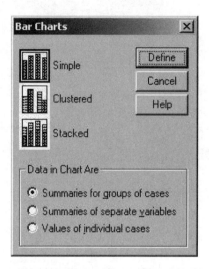

You will be given a small dialog box that precedes the main "Bar Chart" dialog boxes. For this example, click "Simple," then click the "Define" key. Now you will be given the "Define Simple Bar" dialog box and can enter the information to produce the graph.

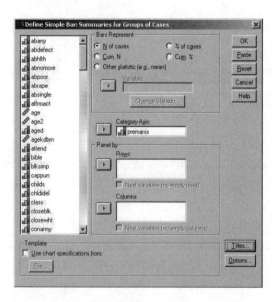

In this example, select "N of cases," indicating that the frequency count will be displayed. Then select the variable for graphing from the list on the left and click the arrow, moving it into the "Category Axis" box. Then click "OK." Following is an image of the graph that SPSS will produce.

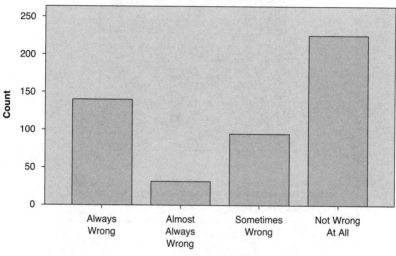

SOURCE: General Social Survey, 2002.[1]

One might wish to produce clustered bar graphs when comparing the information, such as that shown above about beliefs concerning premarital sex, across categories like gender, race/ethnicity, or age groups. In the example that follows, we examine beliefs about premarital sex by gender. With a clustered bar graph in this case, it is beneficial to graph the percent of respondents versus the number of respondents so that the relative bar lengths can be more easily compared within categories of the dependent variable. So, select the following menus:

GRAPHS → BAR

Now select the "Clustered" option, as seen in the following image. Then click "Define."

Next you will be presented with the "Define Clustered Bar" dialog box. Here, under "Bars Represent," select "% of cases." Move the dependent variable, "premarsx," into the "Category Axis" box. Next, move the independent variable, "sex," into the "Define Clusters by" box.

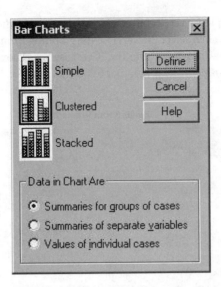

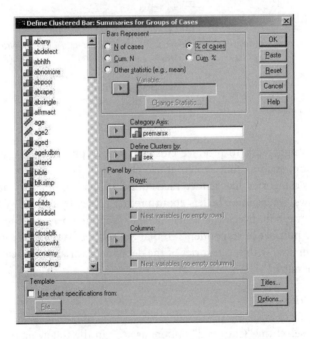

Note that at this stage, one can elect to add titles, subtitles, and footnotes. These can also be added, deleted, or edited later from the output viewer. To add now, click the "Titles" button and you'll be given the dialog box into which you may enter this information.

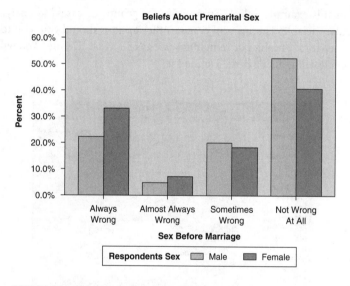

Now, click "Continue" in this box, then click "OK" in the prior dialog box. SPSS will produce the following output.

Beliefs About Premarital Sex

SOURCE: General Social Survey, 2002.[1]

It is readily apparent from the bar chart that has been prepared that females tend to take a less favorable view of premarital sex than do men. Notice that a larger percentage of the women than the men who were in the sample responded "always wrong." Likewise, a smaller percentage of the women responded "not wrong at all."

Pie Chart

Pie charts are circular graphs with slices that represent the proportion of the total contained within each category. In order to produce a pie chart, select the following menus:

GRAPHS → PIE

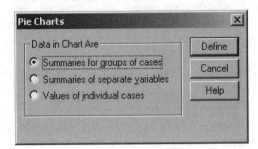

For this example, select "Summaries for groups of cases" to analyze one particular variable. There are, of course, other options should you wish to summarize separate variables or individual cases. Next, click "Define." You will then see the following dialog box: "Define Pie."

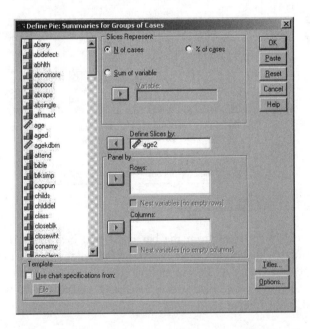

For this example, select "age2" and move it into the "Define Slices by" box. Remember that "age2" is a recoded dichotomy of age into "under 50," and "50 and over." Therefore, it is appropriate to make a pie chart. It would be of little or no use to create a pie chart for the original age variable, since there would be too many slices to make sense from.

**Age Dichotomized Under 50,
50 & Over**

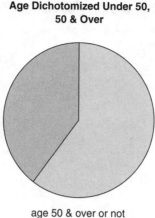

age 50 & over or not

| ▨ .00 | ▢ 1.00 |

SOURCE: General Social Survey, 2002.[1]

The SPSS output above provides descriptive (frequency) information in visual form for the variable selected, "age2."

Alternate Methods of Creating Charts and Graphs

Many functions in SPSS can be performed by employing different techniques through the "point-and-click" interface. Many graphs can be produced by also selecting the following menus:

GRAPHS → INTERACTIVE → PIE → SIMPLE

The following dialog box will be given that will allow you to select the information needed for the pie chart. Note that bar graphs and many other types of graphs can be created this way; to see which ones look at the list in the "Interactive" menu.

There are a number of active options that can be selected in this dialog box. As is, the chart produced will look like the one produced in the previous section. In addition to adding titles, by clicking on the "Titles" tab you can also select "Pies," which will allow you to choose the orientation and direction of the slice assignments in the pie chart. Chart styles, axes, and more can be customized under the "Options" tab. By clicking on the "2-D Coordinate" button, you may also request a 3-D effect chart. Other graphs, such as bar graphs, allow similar customization using the interactive interface.

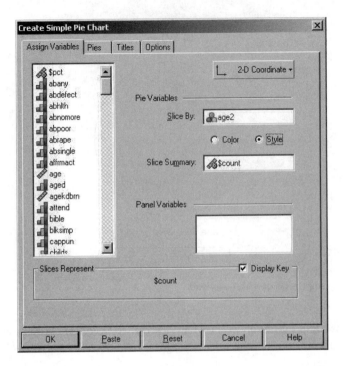

Note

1. Davis, James Allan, Tom W. Smith, and Peter V. Marsden. 2002. GENERAL SOCIAL SURVEY 2002 [UNITED STATES] [computer file]. Chicago, IL: National Opinion Research Center [produce]; Storrs, CT: The Roper Center for Public Opinion Research, University of Connecticut [distributor].

5

Cross-Tabulation and Measures of Association for Nominal and Ordinal Variables

T he most basic type of cross-tabulation (crosstabs) is used to analyze relationships between two variables. This allows a researcher to explore the relationship between variables by examining the intersections of categories of each of the variables involved. The simplest type of cross-tabulation is bivariate analysis, an analysis of two variables. However, the analysis can be expanded beyond that.

Bivariate Analysis

By example, follow these menus to conduct a cross-tabulation of two variables:

ANALYZE → DESCRIPTIVES → CROSSTABS . . .

After selecting those menus, you will be presented with a dialog box like the one above. Here, you will have the opportunity to select the row and column variables for the bivariate table. As is customary, it is recommended that you choose the independent variable as the column variable. Above, "cappun" (view on capital punishment/the death penalty) has been selected for the row

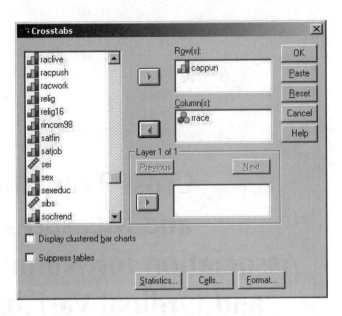

variable, and "rrace" (recoded version of respondent's race) has been chosen as the column variable. We use "rrace" because the number of categories has been collapsed to four. This makes it easier to interpret data from cross-tabulations when the number of categories is kept smaller. Next, click on the "Cells" button to choose options about what information will be given in the output table.

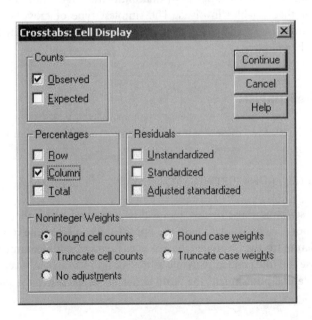

Be sure that the "Column" box is checked under "Percentages." This will ensure that you have information from the appropriate perspective to analyze your variables based on which is the predictor. Click "Continue" in the "Cell Display" dialog box, then "OK" in the original "Crosstabs" dialog box. The table that follows comes from the output produced by following the aforementioned steps.

FAVOR OR OPPOSE DEATH PENALTY FOR MURDER * Race Cross-Tabulation

			Race				
			other	white	black	Hispanic	Total
FAVOR OR OPPOSE DEATH PENALTY FOR MURDER	FAVOR	Count	14	412	45	14	485
		% within race recode	58.3%	71.4%	48.4%	82.4%	68.2%
	OPPOSE	Count	10	165	48	3	226
		% within race recode	41.7%	28.6%	51.6%	17.6%	31.8%
Total		Count	24	577	93	17	711
		% within race recode	100.0%	100.0%	100.0%	100.0%	100.0%

Based on the information in the table, it is easy to see that there is some sort of relationship between the variables of interest in this case. Note that by looking at the percentages across the columns (categories of the independent variable), one can see that there are differences in opinion by race about the death penalty. According to these GSS (General Social Survey) data, whites and Hispanics are more likely to favor the death penalty than blacks or others.

Adding Another Variable or Dimension to the Analysis

Suppose we want to further explore the bivariate relationship that we briefly examined in the preceding section. By adding another variable, such as respondent's sex, we can further explore how opinions about capital punishment are held in the United States. One way that we can perform this type of analysis is to split our data file by respondent's sex. At that point, any analysis that we do will be performed across the categories of the variable with which we have split the data set.

In order to split the data file by respondent's sex, use these menus:

DATA → SPLIT FILE . . .

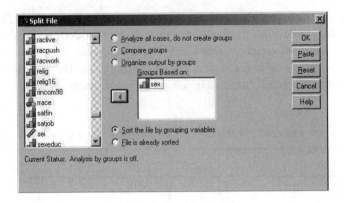

You will be given a "Split File" dialog box like the one above. Here, choose the "Compare groups" radio button. This will brighten the "Groups Based on" box and allow you to now move variables into that box, which will then be used to split the data file. Find "sex" from the variable bank on the left and move it over into the "Groups Based on" box. It is often a good idea to make sure that the file is sorted by grouping variables, although this is not necessary. Click "OK."

SPSS will now perform the "Split File" function. You will know that the data file has been split by the indicator in the lower right-hand window of the data editor. It will say "Split File On."

Now go back to the "Crosstabs" menu and perform the same operations that were done in the previous section. (The variables and setting should remain the same from before, so unless you've restarted SPSS in between, it will just be a matter of choosing "OK" once the dialog box appears.)

ANALYZE → DECRIPTIVES → CROSSTABS . . .

FAVOR OR OPPOSE DEATH PENALTY FOR MURDER * Race Cross-Tabulation

R's SEX				Race				Total
				other	white	black	Hispanic	
MALE	FAVOR OR OPPOSE DEATH PENALTY FOR MURDER	FAVOR	Count	9	225	19	8	261
			% race	64.3%	78.1%	59.4%	80.0%	75.9%
		OPPOSE	Count	5	63	13	2	83
			% race	35.7%	21.9%	40.6%	20.0%	24.1%
	Total		Count	14	288	32	10	344
			% race	100.0%	100.0%	100.0%	100.0%	100.0%
FEMALE	FAVOR OR OPPOSE DEATH PENALTY FOR MURDER	FAVOR	Count	5	187	26	6	224
			% race	50.0%	64.7%	42.6%	85.7%	61.0%
		OPPOSE	Count	5	102	35	1	143
			% race	50.0%	35.3%	57.4%	14.3%	39.0%
	Total		Count	10	289	61	7	367
			% race	100.0%	100.0%	100.0%	100.0%	100.0%

The preceding table is presented as part of the output that SPSS returns. Although it is similar to the table given in the prior section, note that it has twice as many cells. It has been split into two tables, one for males and one for females. In this instance, among other things, it can be seen from the table that Hispanic females have the highest percentage of all categories of men and women who "favor the death penalty for murder." In all other racial categories, men tend to be more likely to favor the death penalty. By adding this new dimension, we are able to obtain some additional insight into public opinion on this matter. See your statistics or research methods book(s) for more details.

Measures of Association for Nominal and Ordinal Variables

PRE statistics allow us to determine the proportional reduction of error achieved by adding one or more variables to an analysis (even if just one independent variable). "PRE measures are derived by comparing the errors made in predicting the dependent variable while ignoring the independent variable with errors made when making predictions that use information about the independent variable" (Frankfort-Nachmias & Leon-Guerrero, 2006). For nominal variables, we utilize lambda. For details on how lambda is calculated, see Chapter 7 of *Social Statistics for a Diverse Society* (2006).

Lambda

To compute lambda for the relationship between race and view on capital punishment, being again by selecting the cross-tabulation menu:

ANALYZE → DESCRIPTIVES → CROSSTABS . . .

Now, when presented the "Crosstabs" dialog box, and after entering the variables of interest, select the "Statistics" button. You will be given the dialog box on the following page.

Under the "Nominal" heading, select "Lambda." This will instruct SPSS to add lambda to the things it will present in the output. Now click "Continue" in the "Statistics" dialog box, then "OK" in the prior dialog box. On the following page you will find an image from the output SPSS would produce.

Typically, lambda is presented as an asymmetrical measure of association as is the case in *Social Statistics for a Diverse Society* (2006). Given that, the value of lambda to be used can be found in the "value" column in the row indicating the correct dependent variable. In this case, "cappun" (Favor or Oppose

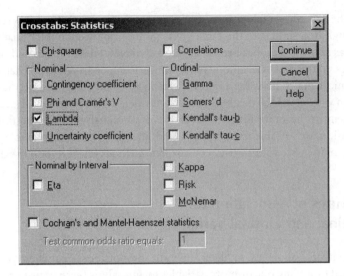

Directional Measures

			Value	Asymp. Std. Error[a]	Approx. T[b]	Approx. Sig.
Nominal by Nominal	Lambda	Symmetric	.008	.027	.311	.756
		FAVOR OR OPPOSE DEATH PENALTY FOR MURDER Dependent	.013	.042	.311	.756
		Race Dependent	.000	.000	.[c]	.[c]
	Goodman and Kruskal tau	FAVOR OR OPPOSE DEATH PENALTY FOR MURDER Dependent	.031	.014		.000[d]
		Race Dependent	.020	.010		.000[d]

a. Not assuming the null hypothesis.

b. Using the asymptotic standard error assuming the null hypothesis.

c. Cannot be computed because the asymptotic standard error equals zero.

d. Based on chi-square approximation

Death Penalty for Murder) is the appropriate dependent variable. We see that lambda is 0.013 and that it is not statistically significant ($p = 0.756$).

Gamma and Somers' d

To compute other measures of association, like gamma and Somers' d, use the following guidelines. Gamma and Somers' d are both measures of association for ordinal variables. Gamma is symmetrical; Somers' d is asymmetrical.

ANALYZE → DESCRIPTIVES → CROSSTABS

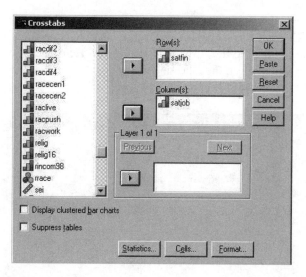

You will be given a "Crosstabs" dialog box. For this example, select "satfin" as the row variable and "satjob" as the column variable. "Satfin" is the variable representing how satisfied the respondent is with her/his financial situation. "Satjob" reveals the level of satisfaction that the respondent feels about her/his job or housework.

Now click the "Cells" button.

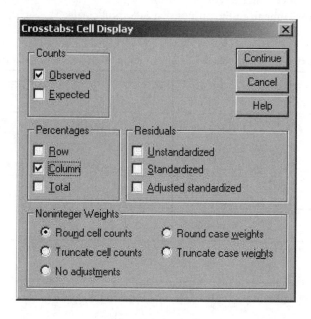

In the "Cells" dialog box, make sure that "Observed" counts are selected and that "Column" percentages have been requested. Now click "Continue." You will be returned to the "Crosstabs" dialog box. Here, click the "Statistics" button. You will be given the following dialog box:

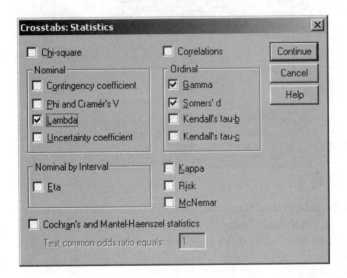

In this box, select "Gamma" and "Somers' d." Click "Continue" and then click "OK" once you are returned to the original "Crosstabs" dialog box. The tables below come from the output that SPSS will create:

SATISFACTION WITH FINANCIAL SITUATION * JOB OR HOUSEWORK Cross-Tabulation

			JOB OR HOUSEWORK				
			VERY SATISFIED	MOD. SATISFIED	A LITTLE DISSAT	VERY DISSATIS FIED	Total
SATISFACTION WITH FINANCIAL SITUATION	SATISFIED	Count	104	53	7	1	165
		% within JOB OR HOUSEWORK	36.6%	26.5%	12.1%	4.0%	29.1%
	MORE OR LESS	Count	117	82	22	9	230
		% within JOB OR HOUSEWORK	41.2%	41.0%	37.9%	36.0%	40.6%
	NOT AT ALL SAT	Count	63	65	29	15	172
		% within JOB OR HOUSEWORK	22.2%	32.5%	50.0%	60.0%	30.3%
Total		Count	284	200	58	25	567
		% within JOB OR HOUSEWORK	100.0%	100.0%	100.0%	100.0%	100.0%

Note that the standard cross-tabulation is produced above and gives an overview by column percents of the relationship between the two variables.

Directional Measures

			Value	Asymp. Std. Error[a]	Approx. T[b]	Approx. Sig.
Nominal by Nominal	Lambda	Symmetric	.024	.023	1.054	.292
		SATISFACTION WITH FINANCIAL SITUATION Dependent	.039	.025	1.504	.133
		JOB OR HOUSEWORK Dependent	.007	.040	.177	.860
	Goodman and Kruskal tau	SATISFACTION WITH FINANCIAL SITUATION Dependent	.031	.009		.000[c]
		JOB OR HOUSEWORK Dependent	.023	.009		.000[c]
Ordinal by Ordinal	Somers' d	Symmetric	.218	.036	6.067	.000
		SATISFACTION WITH FINANCIAL SITUATION Dependent	.227	.037	6.067	.000
		JOB OR HOUSEWORK Dependent	.211	.035	6.067	.000

a. Not assuming the null hypothesis.

b. Using the asymptotic standard error assuming the null hypothesis.

c. Based on chi-square approximation

The value for Somers' *d* is located in the value column in the row with the appropriate variable listed as the dependent variable. (Note that since Somers' *d* is asymmetrical, the two values given, where the dependent variables are different, turn out to be different.) Somers' *d* is statistically significant in this case ($p = 0.000$).

Symmetric Measures

		Value	Asymp. Std. Error[a]	Approx. T[b]	Approx. Sig.
Ordinal by Ordinal	Gamma	.341	.053	6.067	.000
N of Valid Cases		567			

a. Not assuming the null hypothesis.

b. Using the asymptotic standard error assuming the null hypothesis.

Above, note the value for gamma: 0.341. It is also statistically significant ($p = 0.000$).

6

Correlate and Regression Analysis

R egression analysis allows us to predict one variable from information that we have about other variables. In this chapter, linear regression will be addressed. Linear regression is a type of analysis that is performed on interval-ratio variables. First, we will begin with a bivariate regression example and then add some more detail to the analysis.

Bivariate Regression

In the case of bivariate regression, the researcher is interested in predicting the value of the dependent variable, Y, from the information that she or he has about the independent variable, X. We will use the example below, where respondent's occupational prestige score is predicted from number of years of education. Choose the following menus to begin the bivariate regression analysis:

ANALYZE → REGRESSION → LINEAR . . .

The "Linear Regression" dialog box will appear. Initially, just select the variables of interest and move them into the appropriate slots. "Prestg80," respondent's occupational prestige score, should be moved to the "Dependent" slot, and "educ," respondent's number of years of education, should be moved to the "Independent" slot. Now simply click "OK." The following SPSS output will be produced.

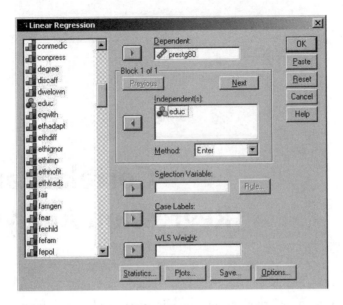

Model Summary

Model	R	R–Square	Adjusted R–Square	Std. Error of the Estimate
1	.481[a]	.231	.230	12.09 i

a. Predictors: (Constant), HIGHEST YEAR OF SCHOOL COMPLETED

In the first column of the model summary, the output will yield Pearson's *r*, as well as *r*-square. SPSS also computes an adjusted *r*-square for those interested in using that value. *R*-square, like lambda, gamma, and Somers' *d*, is a PRE statistic that reveals the proportional reduction in error by introducing the dependent variable(s).

ANOVA[b]

Model		Sum of Squares	df	Mean Square	F	Sig.
1	Regression	62580.057	1	62580.057	428.086	.000[a]
	Residual	208314.8	1425	146.186		
	Total	270894.8	1426			

a. Predictors: (Constant), HIGHEST YEAR OF SCHOOL COMPLETED

b. Dependent Variable: RS OCCUPATIONAL PRESTIGE SCORE (1980)

ANOVA (analysis of variance) values are given in the above table of the linear regression output.

Coefficients[a]

Model		Unstandardized Coefficients		Standardized Coefficients		
		B	Std.Error	Beta	t	Sig.
1	(Constant)	14.056	1.473		9.546	.000
	HIGHEST YEAR OF SCHOOL COMPLETED	2.230	.108	.481	20.690	.000

a. Dependent Variable: RS OCCUPATIONAL PRESTIGE SCORE (1980)

The coefficients table reveals the actual regression coefficients for the regression equation as well as their statistical significance. In the "Unstandardized Coefficients" column, and in the "B" subcolumn, the coefficients are given. In this case, the "b" value for number of years of education completed is 2.230. The "a" value, or constant, is 14.056. By looking in the last column (Sig.), one can see that both values are statistically significant ($p = 0.000$). Therefore, we could write the regression model as follows:

$$\hat{Y} = bX + a \quad \hat{Y} = 2.230 \ X^* + 14.056^*$$

*statistically significant at the $p \leq 0.05$ level

Correlation

Information about correlation tells us the extent to which variables are related. Below, the Pearson method of computing correlation is requested through SPSS. To examine a basic correlation between two variables, use the following menus:

ANALYZE → CORRELATE → BIVARIATE . . .

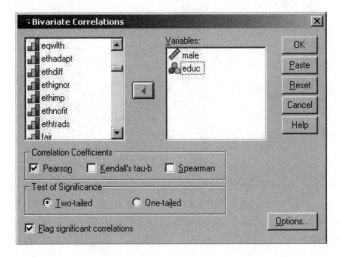

In the "Bivariate Correlations" dialog box, choose the variables that you wish to examine. In the above case, "male" (dummy variable representing sex) and "years of education" have been selected. The output that results is shown as follows:

Correlations

		Male	HIGHEST YEAR OF SCHOOL COMPLETED
Male	Pearson Correlation	1	.021
	Sig. (2-tailed)		.417
	N	1500	1495
HIGHEST YEAR OF SCHOOL COMPLETED	Pearson Correlation	.021	1
	Sig. (2-tailed)	.417	
	N	1495	1495

Note that in the output, the correlation is a low 0.021, which is not statistically significant (*p* value is 0.417).

It is also possible to produce partial correlations. Suppose you are interested in examining the correlation between occupational prestige and education. Further suppose you wish to determine the way that sex impacts that correlation. Follow the following menus to produce a partial correlation:

ANALYZE → CORRELATE → PARTIAL . . .

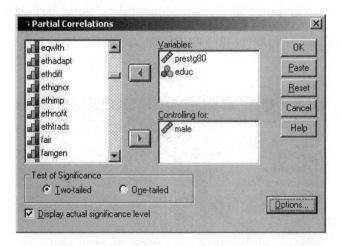

In the "Partial Correlations" dialog box, you will be able to select the variables about which you wish to examine a correlation. You will also be able to select the control variable, around which partial correlations will be computed. In this case, years of education and occupational prestige score have been selected for correlation analysis. The control variable is "male." It is possible to include more than one control variable. SPSS produces the following output:

Correlations

Control Variables			RS OCCUPA-TIONAL PRESTIGE SCORE (1980)	HIGHEST YEAR OF SCHOOL COMPLETED
Male	RS OCCUPATIONAL PRESTIGE SCORE (1980)	Correlation	1.000	.481
		Significance (2-tailed)	.	.000
		df	0	1424
	HIGHEST YEAR OF SCHOOL COMPLETED	Correlation	.481	1.000
		Significance (2-tailed)	.000	.
		df	1424	0

Here the correlation is 0.481 and it is statistically significant (p value is 0.000). Correlation information about variables is useful to have before constructing regression models. Most statistics and research methods books discuss how this information aids in regression analysis.

Multiple Regression

Suppose a researcher wished to do an additional independent variable(s) analysis. It is very easy to do this using SPSS. All one has to do is move the additional variables into the "Independent(s)" slot in the "Linear Regression" dialog box, as seen below.

ANALYZE → REGRESSION → LINEAR . . .

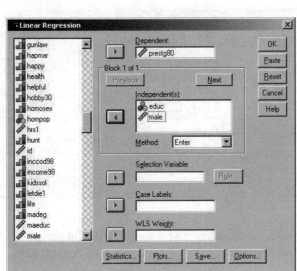

Since linear regression requires interval-ratio variables, one must take care when incorporating variables, such as sex, race/ethnicity, religion, and the like. By creating dummy variables from the categories of these nominal variables, you can add this information to the regression equation.

To do this, use the recode function (see Chapter 1 of this book). Create a dichotomous variable for all but one category, the "omitted" comparison category/attribute, and insert each of those dichotomies into the independent variables slot. The number of dummy variables necessary for a given variable will be equal to $K-1$, where K is the number of categories of the variable. Dichotomies are an exception to the *Cumulative Property of Levels of Measurement,* which tells us that variables measured at higher levels can be treated at lower levels, but *not* vice versa. Dichotomies can be treated as any level of measurement.

For the case of sex, we already have a dichotomy exclusive of transgender and other conditions, so the recode just changes this to one variable: "male" (alternatively, you could have changed it to "female"). The coding should be binary: 1 for affirmation of the attribute, 0 for respondents not possessing the attribute. Now, as was entered into the previous dialog box, just select the newly recoded variable, "male," from the variable bank on the left and move it into the "Independent(s)" slot on the right. You may need to set the variable property to scale in the "Variable View" window so that SPSS will allow that variable to be included in the regression analysis. SPSS 14.0 tracks variable types and often will not allow you to include variables with a lower level of measurement in analyses requiring variables with higher levels of measurement.

Now click the "Plots" button, and you will be given the following ("Plots") dialog box:

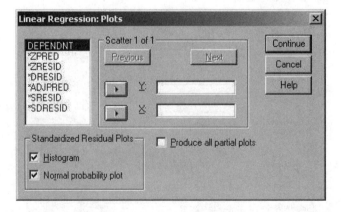

Here you can avail yourself of a couple of useful graphics: a histogram and a normal probability plot. Click each box to request them. Then click "Continue."

When you are returned to the "Linear Regression" dialog box, select the "Statistics" button. The following dialog box will appear:

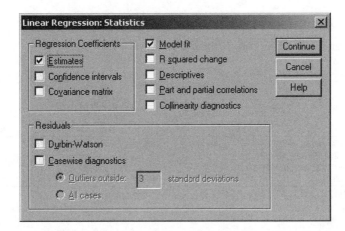

There are a number of options, including descriptive statistics, that you may select to be included in the SPSS linear regression output. Click "Continue" in this box, then click "OK" when returned to the "Linear Regression" dialog box. Below, find tables from the SPSS output. The first two tables give the same sort of information as before in the bivariate regression case: Pearson's r (correlation coefficient), r-square (PRE), and ANOVA (analysis of variance) values.

Model Summary[b]

Model	R	R–Square	Adjusted R–Square	Std. Error of the Estimate
1	.481[a]	.231	.230	12.091

a. Predictors: (Constant), Male, HIGHEST YEAR OF SCHOOL COMPLETED

b. Dependent Variable: RS OCCUPATIONAL PRESTIGE SCORE (1980)

ANOVA[b]

Model		Sum of Squares	df	Mean Square	F	Sig.
1	Regression	62711.973	2	31355.986	214.479	.000[a]
	Residual	208182.9	1424	146.196		
	Total	270894.8	1426			

a. Predictors: (Constant), Male, HIGHEST YEAR OF SCHOOL COMPLETED

b. Dependent Variable: RS OCCUPATIONAL PRESTIGE SCORE (1980)

The "Coefficients" table again provides the information that can be used to construct the regression model/equation. Note that the dummy variable, "male," was not statistically significant.

$$\hat{Y} = bX_1 + bX_2 + a \qquad \hat{Y} = 2.231X_1{}^* - 0.611X_2 + 14.317^*$$

*statistically significant at the $p \leq 0.05$ level

Coefficients[a]

Model		Unstandardized Coefficients		Standardized Coefficients		
		B	Std. Error	Beta	t	Sig.
1	(Constant)	14.317	1.498		9.558	.000
	HIGHEST YEAR OF SCHOOL COMPLETED	2.231	.108	.481	20.699	.000
	Male	−.611	.643	−.022	−.950	.342

a. Dependent Variable: RS OCCUPATIONAL PRESTIGE SCORE (1980)

The two graphics that follow show a histogram of the regression standardized residual for the dependent variable as well as the observed by expected cumulative probability for the dependent variable, "occupational prestige."

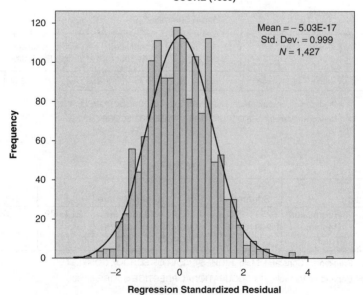

Histogram

Dependent Variable: RS OCCUPATIONAL PRESTIGE SCORE (1980)

Mean = − 5.03E-17
Std. Dev. = 0.999
N = 1,427

**Normal P-Plot of Regression Standardized
Residual**

**Dependent Variable:
RS OCCUPATIONAL PRESTI...**

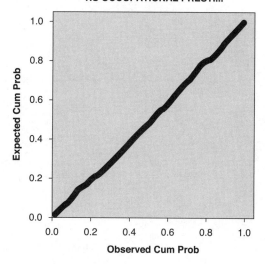

It is possible to add additional variables to the linear regression model you wish to create, as in the dialog box featured below. Interval-ratio variables may be included, as well as dummy variables and others such as interaction variables. Interaction variables may be computed using the "Compute" function (in the "Transform" menu). More information about computing variables can be found in Chapter 1. The computation would consist of variable1* variable2 = interaction variable.

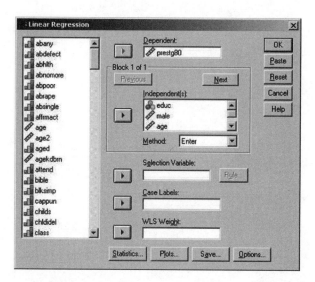

7

Selecting and Sampling Cases

T he SPSS software allows a user to draw a sample from a data set. This could be a random or a targeted sample.

Targeted Selection

For a particular analysis, researchers may not be interested in including all of the cases from a particular data file. There are numerous reasons why this might occur. For instance, if the researcher is interested in studying character-istics of only persons over 21 years of age, then she or he will need to eliminate any cases in the data set of individuals who are 21 years of age or under.

This condition comes up most often when using a secondary data set, one created by a third party, such as the GSS (General Social Survey). Since it was not originally custom-tailored to the needs of the researcher, that researcher will need to select the appropriate cases (as well as possibly recode variables, etc.).

To begin, select the following menus:

DATA → SELECT CASES . . .

After choosing those menus, you will be given the "Select Cases" dialog box. Here you can choose the types of respondents you would like to analyze and hence ignore those who do not fit your criteria for inclusion. To do so, click the "If" button under "Select . . . If condition is satisfied." Then choose the corresponding radio button. Once you do that, you will be presented with the "If" dialog box, like the one that follows:

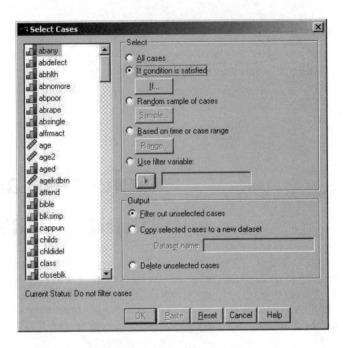

The functions in this box are similar in nature and operation to the functions in the "Compute" dialog box used to compute new variables from existing data, described in Chapter 1. Suppose, as described earlier, the user wished to include only those respondents who were over 21 years of age (i.e., 22 years of age and older).

First, select the necessary variable(s) from the variable bank on the left. In this case, we need the variable "age." Click the arrow to move it to the right side of the dialog box. Now click the "greater than" sign and enter the number 21. Alternatively, you could have selected the "greater than or equal to" button and entered the number 22. Since age is measured in whole years in the GSS, these two methods will return the same outcome.

Click "Continue" in the "If" dialog box, then click "OK" in the "Select Cases" dialog box. Next, see the "Data View" window of your data set.

	abany	abdefect	abhlth	abnomore	abpoor	abrape	absingle	affrmact	age	aged	agekdbrn
1	1	1	1	1	1	1	1	0	43	1	24
2	0	0	0	0	0	0	0	0	37	0	22
3	2	1	1	2	2	2	2	0	46	1	29
4	0	0	0	0	0	0	0	0	52	0	28
5	0	0	0	0	0	0	0	0	48	0	29
6	0	0	0	0	0	0	0	3	37	1	0
7	0	0	0	0	0	0	0	0	28	0	0
8	0	0	0	0	0	0	0	3	33	1	33
9	2	1	1	8	8	1	8	4	57	0	0
10	2	1	1	2	2	1	2	0	63	1	0
11	0	0	0	0	0	0	0	0	43	0	0
12	0	0	0	0	0	0	0	4	20	2	0
13	1	1	1	1	1	1	1	0	71	1	24
14	1	1	1	1	1	1	1	0	53	2	23
15	0	0	0	0	0	0	0	0	48	0	24
16	2	1	2	2	2	2	2	4	45	0	22
17	0	0	0	0	0	0	0	0	49	0	0
18	1	1	1	2	8	8	2	0	62	2	19
19	0	0	0	0	0	0	0	0	76	0	26
20	0	0	0	0	0	0	0	0	78	0	19
21	0	0	0	0	0	0	0	0	29	0	20
22	0	0	0	0	0	0	0	0	44	0	30
23	0	0	0	0	0	0	0	0	44	0	0
24	0	0	0	0	0	0	0	0	38	0	23
25	0	0	0	0	0	0	0	0	74	0	18
26	0	0	0	0	0	0	0	3	50	2	29
27	0	0	0	0	0	0	0	1	21	1	0
28	0	0	0	0	0	0	0	0	50	0	22
29	2	2	1	2	2	2	2	0	21	1	0

Note that some of the cases have a diagonal line through the SPSS case number at the left. This is how SPSS lets you know which cases will be omitted from any and all analyses performed until the "Select Cases" function is changed or turned off.

Random Selection

Suppose the user wants to select a random group of cases from a particular data set. This can also be done by calling up the "Select Cases" dialog box:

DATA → SELECT CASES . . .

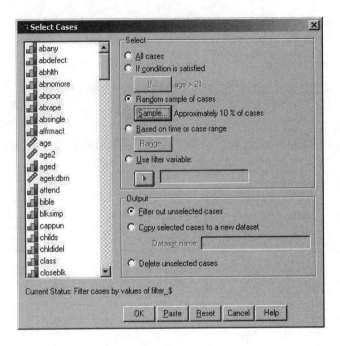

This time, click the "Sample" button after choosing the corresponding radio button "Select . . . Random sample of cases." You will then be given the "Random Sample" dialog box seen here:

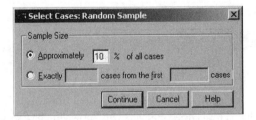

For this example, 10% of the cases will be chosen. SPSS uses the word *approximately,* since not all data sets are necessarily divisible by the percentage that you choose, and hence would not return a whole number of cases in the sample. Note that alternatively, you could select the other radio button and choose an exact number of cases from the first N number of cases as the file is sorted. (Use the DATA → SORT CASES menu to change the way the cases in your data set are ordered by SPSS.)

Click "Continue," then click "OK" when you are taken back to the "Select Cases" dialog box. The screen image below shows the variable view, the "Data Editor" window, after this action was performed:

Many (approximately 90%) of the cases have a diagonal line through the SPSS case number at the left. Again, this is how SPSS lets you know which cases will be omitted from any and all analyses performed until the "Select Cases" function is changed or turned off.

Selecting Cases for Inclusion in a New Data Set

Up to this point, we have selected cases from a data set while having SPSS ignore those cases that were not selected for inclusion. It is also possible to have SPSS create a new data file that contains only the cases that have been selected.

The process of case selection is identical. The difference is in the "Output" section of the dialog box:

DATA → SELECT CASES . . .

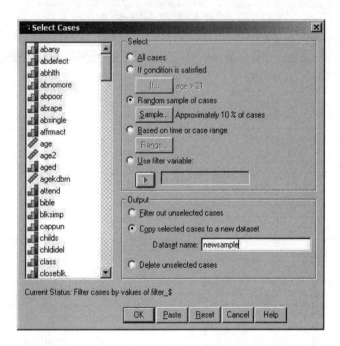

Choose the radio button for "Copy selected cases to a new dataset." Then enter a name for your new file. It will be stored in the default directory as an SPSS *.sav file. The advantage to choosing this option is that you can work with the subset data file without risk of altering the original data file.

8

Testing Hypotheses Using Means and Cross-Tabulation

S PSS allows for automatic testing of hypotheses without having to make a computation and check a cut point in a table in the back of a statistics book. The actual statistical significance is presented with the results.

Comparing Means

This section explains how to examine differences between two means. Comparing means between groups requires having a variable that will allow for a division into the appropriate groups, in the same way that it is required to split a data file for a comparative analysis.

Suppose you are interested in comparing the occupational prestige scores of respondents and wish to examine the differences between men and women. Select the following menus:

ANALYZE → COMPARE MEANS → MEANS . . .

Additional layers can be requested by clicking "Next," then adding the additional variable(s). The DATA → SPLIT FILE option can also be used to compare groups across categories/attributes of a variable. By clicking on the "Options" button, you can customize the cell statistics that SPSS will report in the output.

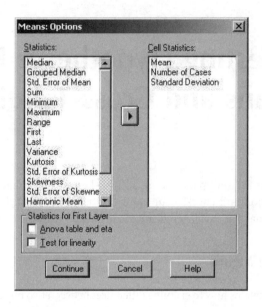

After clicking "Continue" and then "OK" in the "Means" dialog box, SPSS will generate the following output:

Report

RS OCCUPATIONAL PRESTIGE SCORE (1980)

Male	Mean	N	Std. Deviation
.00	43.98	785	13.588
1.00	43.51	645	14.025
Total	43.77	1430	13.784

A simple table is provided, yielding mean, sample size, and standard deviation for the total sample, as well as each category of the variable of interest, "occupational prestige."

Comparing Means: Paired-Samples *t*-Test

The paired-samples *t*-test can be used when two pieces of information (variables) from the same case are to be compared, collectively. An example of such a situation would be a data file containing a group of people who have taken a particular pretest and then an identical posttest after some sort of stimulus has been administered. There are many situations where this method of analysis is appropriate.

From the General Social Survey (GSS), we can compare parental education by parent's gender. In other words, we can compare the years of education completed of the respondents' fathers and mothers. To begin, select the following menus:

ANALYZE → COMPARE MEANS → PAIRED SAMPLES T-TEST . . .

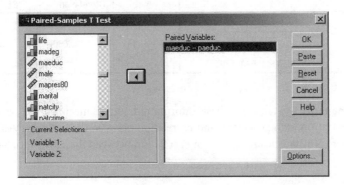

In order to move a selection into the "Paired Variables" box, you will need to select two variables from the variable bank on the left side of the dialog box. Once you have selected two variables, their names will appear in the "Current Selections" area. After the intended selections have been made, click the arrow to move them over into the "Paired Variables" box.

Should you wish to change the confidence interval (default is 95%), or change the way that missing cases are handled/excluded, click the "Options" key and you will be given a dialog box to make those selections:

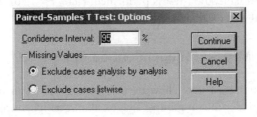

Click "Continue" in the "Options" box, then click "OK" in the "Paired-Samples T Test" box. What follows is output that SPSS will produce to fulfill your request.

Paired-Samples Statistics

		Mean	N	Std. Deviation	Std. Error Mean
Pair 1	HIGHEST YEAR SCHOOL COMPLETED, MOTHER	11.55	1021	3.544	.111
	HIGHEST YEAR SCHOOL COMPLETED, FATHER	11.38	1021	4.128	.129

Paired-Samples Correlations

		N	Correlation	Sig.
Pair 1	HIGHEST YEAR SCHOOL COMPLETED, MOTHER & HIGHEST YEAR SCHOOL COMPLETED, FATHER	1021	.660	.000

The above two tables give basic information, such as mean, sample size, standard deviation, standard error, and correlation between the two variables. Note that there is a statistically significant correlation between these two variables.

Paired-Samples Test

		Paired Differences						
				95% Confidence Interval of the Difference				
		Mean	Std. Deviation	Lower	Upper	t	df	Sig. (2-tailed)
Pair 1	MA-Ed & PA-Ed	.171	3.209	-.026	.368	1.707	1020	.088

In the third table, the t-test is performed. Here, $t = 1.707$. It is not, however, significant at the 0.05 level or better.

Comparing Means: Independent-Samples t-Test

Independent-samples t-tests allow us to compare the mean of a particular variable across independent groups. To look at an example using occupational prestige scale scores, use the following menu selections:

ANALYZE → COMPARE MEANS → INDEPENDENT-SAMPLES T TEST . . .

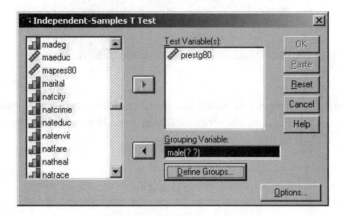

In this dialog box, move the variable of interest, "occupational prestige score," into the "Test Variable(s)" box. Next, you will need to select the grouping variable. "Male" (dummy variable for gender) has been selected. Now we need to inform SPSS which groups are to be compared. Click the "Define Groups" button.

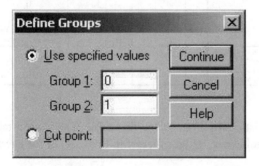

In this "Define Groups" dialog box, fill in the category values for each group. Note that depending on how the grouping variable is categorized, you have the option of selecting a cut point to define the groups. This could be done with age, test scores, and so on.

Click "Continue," which will take you back to the "Independent-Samples T Test" dialog box. You have the option of changing the confidence interval and method of case exclusion. To make those choices, click the "Options" button and you will be given the dialog box that follows:

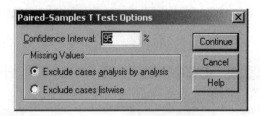

Enter the changes you would like to make, if any, then click "Continue," and then click "OK" in the original dialog box. The output below will be generated by SPSS in response to your query.

Group Statistics

	Male	N	Mean	Std. Deviation	Std. Error Mean
RS OCCUPATIONAL PRESTIGE SCORE (1980)	.00	785	43.98	13.588	.485
	1.00	645	43.51	14.025	.552

Independent-Samples Test

		Levene's Test for Equality of Variances		t-test for Equality of Means						
									95% Confidence Interval of the Difference	
		F	Sig.	t	df	Sig. (2-tailed)	Mean Difference	Std. Error Difference	Lower	Upper
RS OCCUPATIONAL PRESTIGE SCORE (1980)	Equal variances assumed	.739	.390	.654	1428	.513	.479	.733	-.958	1.917
	Equal variances not assumed			.652	1357	.514	.479	.735	-.963	1.921

Basic statistics are given in the first table. The second table reveals the results and significance (or lack thereof in this case) of the *t*-test.

Chi-Square

There are two menu selections that will produce chi-square results. The first is demonstrated here. To perform a chi-square analysis, choose the following menu options:

ANALYZE → NONPARAMETRIC TESTS → CHI-SQUARE . . .

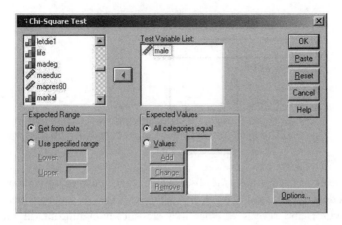

Next, in the "Chi-Square Test" dialog box, choose the variable that you would like to test. In this case, we chose "male," the dummy variable representing gender. For expected values, by leaving the button selected for "All categories equal," the expectation is that 50% of the respondents will be men and 50% will be women.

By clicking on the "Options" button, you will be given a dialog box that allows you to request additional information and determine the method by which cases should be excluded.

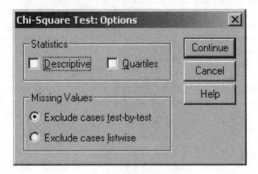

When these decisions have been made, click "Continue," then click "OK" in the "Chi-Square Test" dialog box. The output that follows will be provided by SPSS:

Male

	Observed N	Expected N	Residual
.00	832	750.0	82.0
1.00	668	750.0	-82.0
Total	1500		

Test Statistics

	Male
Chi-Square[a]	17.931
df	1
Asymp. Sig.	.000

a. 0 cells (.0%) have expected frequencies less than
5. The minimum expected cell frequency is 750.0.

The first table provides the observed and expected amounts, and of course the residual or difference. The second table yields the chi-square value, degrees of freedom, and reveals whether it is statistically significant. In this case, chi-square = 17.931 with 1 degree of freedom and is statistically significant.

If you would like to produce full cross-tabulations, such as those detailed in Chapter 3, included with the chi-square information, see the following example by selecting the following menus:

ANALYZE → DESCRIPTIVES → CROSSTABS . . .

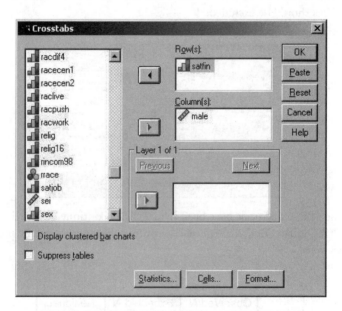

Click the "Statistics" button and you will be presented with the following dialog box:

Select the "Chi-square" option. This will produce the following SPSS output:

SATISFACTION WITH FINANCIAL SITUATION * Male Cross-Tabulation

Count

		Male		
		.00	1.00	Total
SATISFACTION	SATISFIED	117	111	228
WITH FINANCIAL	MORE OR LESS	151	145	296
SITUATION	NOT AT ALL SAT	123	97	220
Total		391	353	744

Chi-Square Tests

	Value	df	Asymp. Sig. (2-sided)
Pearson Chi-Square	1.415[a]	2	.493
Likelihood Ratio	1.418	2	.492
Linear-by-Linear Association	.931	1	.335
N of Valid Cases	744		

a. 0 cells (.0%) have expected count less than 5. The minimum expected count is 104.38.

Note that the chi-square value of 1.415 (2 degrees of freedom) is not statistically significant according to the results presented in this output.

9

Analysis of Variance

A nalysis of variance (ANOVA) involves a statistical test for significance of differences between mean scores of at least two groups across one or more than one variable. ANOVA can be used to test for statistical significance using categorical independent variables in conjunction with a continuous dependent variable.

One-Way ANOVA

To perform a one-way ANOVA test, use the following menus:

ANALYZE → COMPARE MEANS → ONE-WAY ANOVA . . .

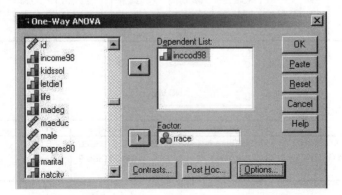

In the dialog box that is presented, choose the dependent and independent (factor) variables for your analysis. Click the "Options" key to customize your selections further. You will be given the following dialog box:

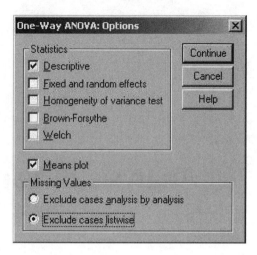

Here, descriptive statistics have been requested as well as a plot of the means. Cases have been excluded listwise. The output that follows begins with the descriptive statistic information and is followed next by the ANOVA results.

Descriptives

Rincome98 Recode

	N	Mean	Std. Deviation	Std. Error	95% Confidence Interval for Mean		Minimum	Maximum
					Lower Bound	Upper Bound		
other	34	28433.82	23135.660	3967.733	20361.41	36506.24	500	100000
white	742	36283.69	26662.234	978.801	34362.14	38205.25	500	110000
black	129	25362.40	16543.059	1456.535	22480.40	28244.41	500	110000
Hispanic	29	28551.72	17168.984	3188.200	22020.99	35082.46	500	82500
Total	934	34249.46	25423.650	831.887	32616.88	35882.05	500	110000

ANOVA

Rincome98 Recode

	Sum of Squares	df	Mean Square	F	Sig.
Between Groups	15350260878.621	3	5116753626	8.097	.000
Within Groups	587705488853.72	930	631941385.9		
Total	603055749732.34	933			

The means plot has also been provided as requested. It is provided initially as a line graph, which might be useful as a visual tool for a ranked categorical variable, but in this case using race, it would be more beneficial to provide this graphic as a bar chart. Double-click the graph to open the "Chart Editor" window. Here, follow these menus to convert the graph:

TRANSFORM → SIMPLE BAR

Then use these menus:

FILE → CLOSE

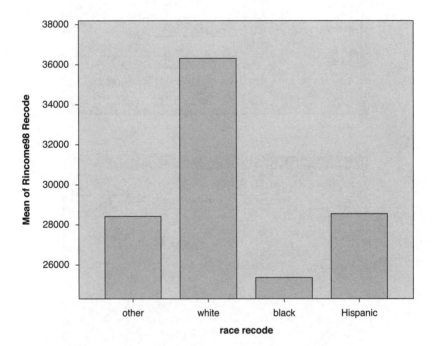

ANOVA in Regression

To examine ANOVA in a regression model, use the following menus:

ANALYZE → REGRESSION → LINEAR . . .

When presented with the "Linear Regression" dialog box, enter your dependent variable and independent variables. To obtain additional partial correlation values or estimates, click the "Statistics" button and mark the appropriate boxes in that dialog box.

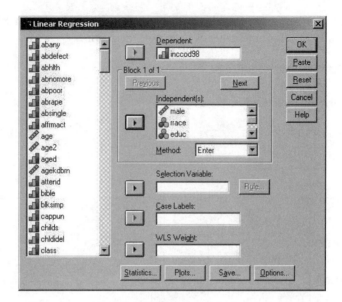

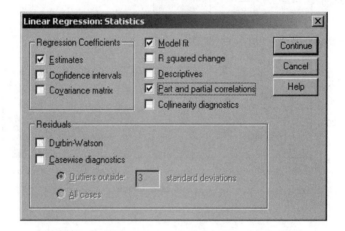

After clicking "Continue" in the above dialog box, then "OK" in the "Linear Regression" dialog box, the following output will be presented. Note that the sum of squares and mean squares have been provided, as well as the F statistic and its *p* value (indicating whether it is statistically significant).

Model Summary

Model	R	R-Square	Adjusted R-Square	Std. Error of the Estimate
1	.441[a]	.194	.192	22858.666

a. Predictors: (Constant), HIGHEST YEAR OF SCHOOL COMPLETED, Male, race recode

ANOVA[b]

Model		Sum of Squares	df	Mean Square	F	Sig.
1	Regression	117113428114	3	39037809371	74.711	.000[a]
	Residual	485942321618	930	522518625.396		
	Total	603055749732	933			

a. Predictors: (Constant), HIGHEST YEAR OF SCHOOL COMPLETED, Male, race recode

b. Dependent Variable: Rincome98 Recode

Coefficients[a]

Model		Unstandardized Coefficients		Standardized Coefficients	t	Sig.	Correlations		
		B	Std. Error	Beta			Zero-order	Partial	Part
1	(Constant)	-11905.2	4394.598		-2.709	.007			
	Male	13670.6	1499.218	.269	9.118	.000	.272	.286	.268
	race recode	-2329.32	1447.081	-.048	-1.610	.108	-.103	-.053	-.047
	HIGHEST YEAR OF SCHOOL COMPLETED	3082.914	270.402	.338	11.401	.000	.344	.350	.336

a. Dependent Variable: Rincome98 Recode

10

Editing Output

The SPSS Output Editor allows a great degree of freedom for editing charts, tables, and other output. This information can all be exported to other computer programs for inclusion in other documents. A popular feature is that the information can be suitably imported and handled within Microsoft Word as well as other computer word-processing programs.

Editing Basic Tables

The first table below was produced by default by SPSS for a "Compare Means" function request. The second table has been edited. Labels have been added/edited and at least one column was resized. There are at least two ways to edit tables in SPSS. First, you can click on the table and move cells, double-click and retype labels, and so on. This is done much the same way that table editing is done using a spreadsheet, such as Microsoft Excel.

Report

RS OCCUPATIONAL PRESTIGE SCORE (1980)

Male	Mean	N	Std. Deviation
.00	43.98	785	13.588
1.00	43.51	645	14.025
Total	43.77	1430	13.784

Job Prestige by Gender

RS OCCUPATIONAL PRESTIGE SCORE (1980)

FEMALE	Mean	N	Std. Deviation
Gender	43.98	785	13.588
MALE	43.51	645	14.025
Total	43.77	1430	13.784

Alternatively, you can open the table as an object in a new window that offers a greater range of editing options. To do so, follow these menus:

EDIT → SPSS Pivot Table Object → OPEN

SPSS Pivot Table - table10

File   Edit   View   Insert   Pivot   Format   Help

Paired Samples Test

		Paired Differences						
			Std. Deviation	95% Confidence Interval of the Difference		t	df	Sig. (2-tailed)
		Mean		Lower	Upper			
Pair 1	MA-Ed & PA-Ed	.171	3.209	-.026	.368	1.707	1020	.088

The "SPSS Pivot Table" opens in a new window, and you have the option of editing by double-clicking on parts of the table, just as you do directly in the SPSS Output Editor. However, you can also use the menus in this new window that offer more direct control over the features of the table. Explore the menus for options.

Copying to Microsoft Word

There are several options for getting an SPSS table into MS Word. One way is to select the table in the SPSS Output Editor by clicking on it once. Then "copy" the table by choosing the menu:

EDIT → COPY

The keyboard shortcut for that function is <Control> + <C> on a PC and <APPLE> + <C> on a Macintosh computer.

At this point, you can "paste" the output into the word processor (e.g., Microsoft Word).This can be done by selecting the following menus in MS Word:

EDIT → PASTE

Again, there is a keyboard shortcut for this function: <Control> + <V> on a PC and <APPLE> + <V> on a Macintosh computer.

By copying and pasting in this way, you will still have editing functions over the tables in MS Word. It can, however, be a bit more cumbersome to do the table editing in Word, and it can also pose layout complications. It might benefit the user to do the table editing in SPSS, then when editing is complete, copy the table object and then select the following menus in MS Word:

EDIT → PASTE SPECIAL   (Then double-click "Picture.")

This will paste the table into Word as a largely noneditable (but resizable) object. While the internal characteristics of the table can no longer be changed at this point, placement and sizing of the table are much easier this way.

Exporting Output

It is possible to have SPSS automatically export the elements of an output file into separate objects that can be used individually or read into some other program (e.g., a word processor). Follow the following menus:

FILE → EXPORT . . .

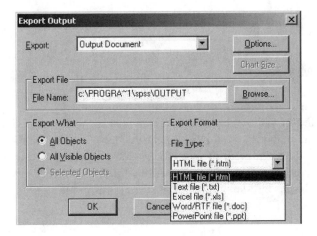

Select what to export: all output, output tables only, or output charts only. Select the format you would like the exported files to be saved in. Also, name the directory where the new files will be saved. By clicking on the "Options" button, you will be given the following dialog box:

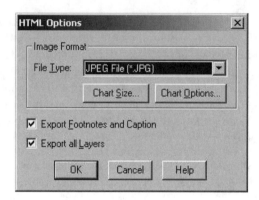

You can choose from the list of file types. By selecting JPEG, all of the charts and tables will be saved as separate *.JPG files, which can be imported into other programs and handled like graphic objects.

Editing Charts and Graphs

The SPSS Output Editor allows for interactive editing of charts and graphs. Not only can labels, titles, numbers, legends, and so on be added and edited, but the very type and style of the chart or graph can be changed from the output interface.

Suppose you create a clustered bar graph, like the one that is created below:

GRAPHS → BAR

Now select "Clustered" and click the "Define" button.

For this graph, the dependent variable that we wish to examine is "cappun," opinion about capital punishment/the death penalty for murder. That variable has been moved into the "Category Axis" slot. The clusters will be defined by gender, so the dummy variable, "male," has been moved into the "Define Clusters by" slot.

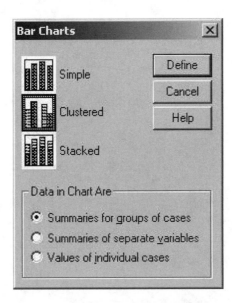

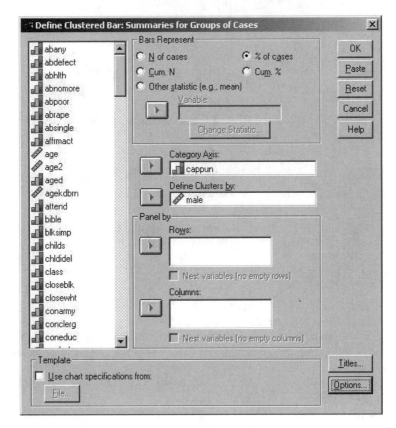

Click "OK" to produce the bar graph seen below. Note that a user can click and double-click on the graph to edit titles, labels, and so forth.

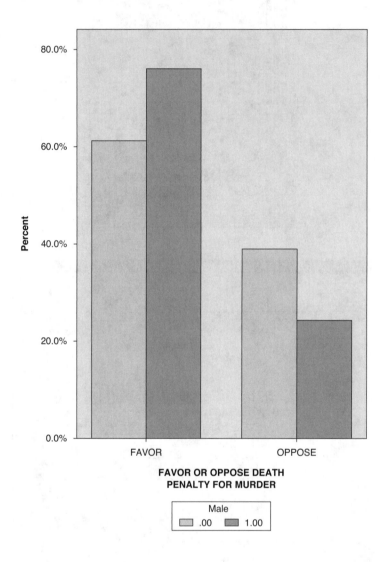

For a more comprehensive and interactive way to edit the bar graph (or any other SPSS chart or graph), select the chart or graph and use the following menus:

EDIT → SPSS CHART OBJECT → OPEN

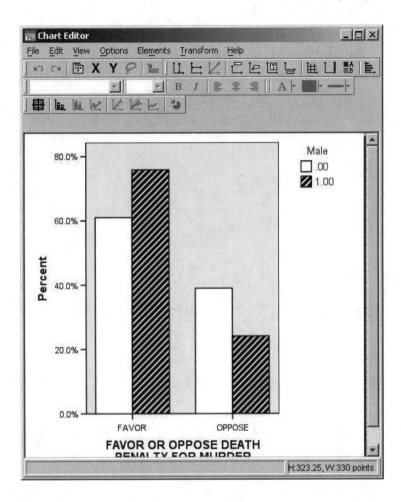

By searching the menu options, you can change any labels, titles, and so on that you may need to change in order to clean up the appearance of the graph or chart.

By selecting "Transform," you can change the clustered bar graph into a stacked bar graph, a line graph, or another type of chart or graph. It is not necessary to go through and rerun the graph/chart function. It can be rebuilt directly from this Editor window.

11

Advanced Applications

Merging Data From Multiple Files

There are typically two ways a user wants to merge files. One way is to combine two data files that contain the same variables but consist of different cases (e.g., two or more waves of surveys completed by different people but including the same information). Another way is to have additional variables to add to existing cases (e.g., second round of responses from the same respondents). Note that you must be doing this from the "Data Editor" window containing the file (active data set) to which you wish to add cases or variables.

First, suppose you want to add cases:

DATA → MERGE FILES → ADD CASES . . .

If you have already opened the data file in another SPSS "Data Editor" window, then you can select "An open dataset" and choose from the list. Otherwise, select "An external SPSS data file" and locate the file you wish to add. Both files, of course, need to be in SPSS (*.sav) format. If the file you are adding is not in SPSS data format, then you should first import that file into SPSS before carrying out the merge function. You will be presented with a new dialog box, like the one that follows:

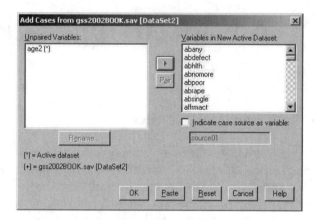

Assuming there are no unpaired variables, or you are not concerned with pairing variables (same variables in two different data sets each with a different name), select "OK" and SPSS will perform the addition of cases to your data file.

Now suppose you want to add variables:

FILE → DATA → ADD VARIABLES . . .

Again select the appropriate file, whether it is open in another instance (window) of SPSS or is located on a disk or server connected to your computer. Click "Continue" and you will be presented with the next dialog box:

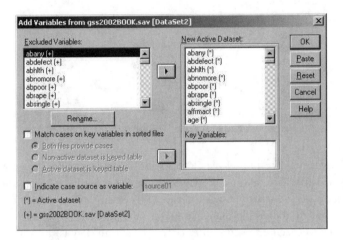

The "New Active Dataset" box shows the variables that will be contained in the newly merged data file. The excluded variables are those that are duplicates in name. If any of those are not duplicates, but happen to have the same name, then select each one and click the "Rename" button to correct the problem. If you are not certain that the cases are in identical order between the two data files, then you must match the cases by some identifying variable (e.g., a case ID); select the variable that contains that information and move it into the "Key Variables" box. Click "OK," and SPSS will perform the merge.

Opening Previously Created Syntax Files

Syntax files provide computer code to instruct SPSS to perform functions. Most of these functions can be achieved by using the "point-and-click" method that this book uses. That is, functions can be performed by using the menus at the top of the "Data Editor" window. Creating syntax code using SPSS syntax computer language is not addressed in this book. If you have an SPSS syntax file, however, with code for performing SPSS tasks, open it as follows:

FILE → OPEN → SYNTAX

You'll get a dialog box like the one on the next page:

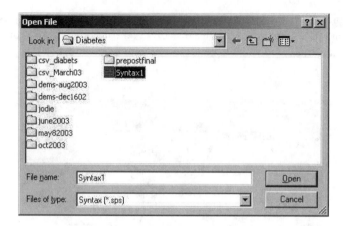

Navigate your computer files, locate your file, and open it. The syntax code will appear in a "Syntax Editor" window, like the one that follows. Select the portion of the code that you wish to run. (The example below runs frequency information on a data file that is supposed to be already opened.) Click the "Run" key to execute the computer code. (The "Run" key is the key with the small blue triangle.) You can also select from the menu:

RUN → ALL

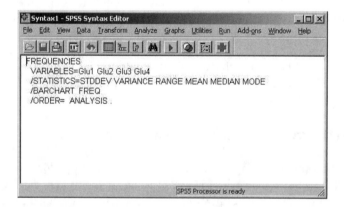

Creating New SPSS Syntax Files

Although this book will not provide detailed information about creating syntax files, there are a few things about syntax files that may be useful, even for those users who have no intention of writing code to perform SPSS functions. To create the new syntax file, select the following menu options:

FILE → OPEN → SYNTAX

A new window, "Syntax Editor," will appear. Whatever information is typed into this interface will comprise the syntax file. All or part of what is typed into this interface can be used at a later time or immediately.

With any of the SPSS "point-and-click" functions (those operations implemented using the menus at the top of the Editor windows) there is an option to select "Paste" instead of clicking "OK." What this does is to not execute the function(s) but instead to record the instructions for performing the functions in a syntax window. A user may choose to save the instructions for use later or run them immediately and save a copy for future use or reference. What is pasted are the instructions that SPSS gives "behind the scenes" for that particular function (e.g., frequency distributions).

Saving pasted SPSS syntax files can be useful for those who are performing many operations that are repetitive or similar across variables—particularly if they are more complicated functions. Saving syntax files also provides a complete record of how a data file was altered, which can be helpful to some users since SPSS will show the altered data file only and not provide a list of updates that have been made.

About the Author

William E. Wagner, III, PhD, is an Assistant Professor of Sociology and Director of Graduate Studies in Sociology at California State University, Bakersfield. He also holds an appointment as a Senior Research Scientist at CSUB's Applied Research Center. His MA and PhD degrees (sociology) are from the University of Illinois, Chicago. His BA degree (mathematics) is from St. Mary's College of Maryland. He teaches courses in research methods and statistics, as well as gay and lesbian studies. His scholarly publications include "Beyond Dollars and Cents: Fashioning Urban Improvements From Civic Capital" in *City and Community* (2004). He is currently working on research involving homophobia in education with a focus on extracurricular activities, as well as research on the social networks of gay professionals.